Exploring Parables in Luke

Exploring Parables in Luke

Integrated Skills for ESL/EFL Students of Theology

Cheri Pierson
Will Bankston
Marilyn Lewis

Published 2014 by Langham Global Library
an imprint of Langham Creative Projects

Langham Partnership
PO Box 296, Carlisle, Cumbria CA3 9WZ, UK
www.langham.org

ISBNs:
978-1-78368-940-8 Print
978-1-78368-913-2 PDF

British Library Cataloguing in Publication Data
Pierson, Cheri author.
Exploring parables in Luke : integrated skills for ESL/EFL students of theology.
1. Jesus Christ--Parables. 2. Bible. Luke--Criticism, interpretation, etc. 3. English language--Textbooks for foreign speakers.
I. Title II. Bankston, Will, author. III. Lewis, Marilyn (Marilyn N.) author.
226.8'06-dc23
ISBN-13: 9781783689408

Cover & Book Design: projectluz.com

Contents

We dedicate this text to the glory of God
and to the teachers and students that will use it around the world.

Acknowledgments

We wish to thank those who assisted us with this project. Special thanks to Ryan Schultz who has served as our research assistant. He has spent endless hours researching, editing and formatting the text. Ryan has a Master of Arts in Intercultural Studies and TESOL from Wheaton College Graduate School. He has taught English as a second language at both the beginning and academic levels in the United States and has a special interest in teaching English language learners internationally.

We are grateful for the help of Daniel Owens, who took time from his busy schedule of new teaching assignments at Singapore Bible College to provide theological editing and insight for many of the textbook's chapters. Given his longstanding experience with the kinds of students this textbook seeks to instruct, his comments always accounted for the particular needs of these theological learners.

We wish to thank Pieter Kwant and Langham Partnership for believing in this project and for preparing the manuscript for publication. Vivian Doub graciously answered many questions throughout the writing of the text.

We also appreciate the assistance of Greg Morrison, Assistant Professor of Library Science, Wheaton College, for his advice throughout the project. We also thank Mary Elizabeth Moore who assisted in editing several sections of the text and checking resources in the library.

We also extend our personal thanks to our families and friends.

Cheri: I want to thank my husband, Dr. Steven Pierson, who provided support each step of the way and was patient when the project took me away from home. Also, I want to thank my colleagues in the Intercultural Studies Department at Wheaton College Graduate School for their encouragement and support.

Will: I want to thank my wife, Kristin, and my sons, Ezra and Oren. They felt the effects of my work on this textbook as I scrambled to finish my chapter contributions in time for our evening walks. They were gracious and flexible with their schedules. Even more, Kristin was always willing, and seemingly excited, to talk over any theological content from the day's work. Through it all, their support kept me encouraged and committed to the textbook's purpose of international theological education.

Marilyn: Thanks to the people in many countries who have brightened my career and life. Thank you as well to the many young nieces and nephews who give my life inspiration.

Cheri Pierson, Will Bankston, Marilyn Lewis

Preface for Teachers

Why parables?

Throughout the world, people tell stories. Some stories entertain; others offer instruction. Many are meant for children; others are meant for adults. We have chosen parables for the topic of this book because they are instructive and offer advice from the storehouse of wisdom to all people. For more than two thousand years, the Lord's parables have clarified and illustrated his teaching concerning the kingdom of God. The biblical parables included in this book also serve as an introduction to similar parables from other cultures and traditions. Some readers may be familiar with the examples that have been included. This book is specifically designed for students of the Bible and theology who speak and read English as a second or foreign language.

What principles are foundational to this book?

As well as building on a genre that will probably be familiar to the students, another of the book's purposes is to avoid the split that often occurs between two parts of students' training in Bible schools and theological seminaries, namely improving their English and doing theological studies. Bringing together language and content has a long history in the language learning field, with English for Academic Purposes (EAP) being one field of English for Specific Purposes (ESP). EAP in its turn has a number of sub-fields, one of which is teaching and learning theological English, an area of study for which one of us has already co-authored a book. We are not the only people to have linked the learning of English with biblical studies. As shown by the list of other titles at the end of this book, others too have used this integrated principle. There are titles devoted specifically to learning theological vocabulary, to writing English for theological purposes, to reading Bible-related texts, and to listening to talks, lectures, and sermons in English.

As well as combining language and content, other principles underpin this book's content and organization. One is learner autonomy. Although many of the tasks go beyond the concept of having just one answer, where there is a right answer, this appears in the key at the end of the book rather than in a separate teacher's guide. The aim is to promote some independence amongst adult learners, rather than insisting that only the teacher could tell them how they are progressing. Learner autonomy is encouraged in other ways throughout the book as well. Students are encouraged to talk in pairs and small groups to one another, not just to the teacher. We know from many studies the advantages of peer interaction.[1]

A further planning principle is that of task-based learning, which has structured language classes for some time now and which continues to be the focus of studies into language learning and teaching. For example, most recently Ellis and Shintani summarize current research into task-based learning with the comment that "a task-based approach is clearly compatible with [the way] learners acquire an L2".[2] In this book of ours the intention will be that learning is active rather than passive. In some of the tasks students can make discoveries for themselves instead of being told information. In other tasks they can try out their new learning in various ways.

We have also planned for integrated skills. Here our aim is to bring together students' development in reading, writing, speaking and listening, as well as providing a focus on vocabulary and grammar. This often happens within the same task.

What is the nature of the theological content?

The theological content of this book is organized in a way that encourages critical thinking through making connections. Each chapter has an article that investigates a specific theological concept, issue, or theme. Students use these articles as a kind of theological compass to navigate the chapters, especially as they work to interpret the parables of Jesus. Along the way, students will bring together ideas and information, which at first, might not seem directly related. This ongoing process of connecting various kinds of content aims to cultivate critical thinking that understands theology as:

- *comprehensive* (necessary for every area of life)
- *cohesive* (comprising a unity corresponding to the unified, biblical testimony of the Triune God)
- *creative* (requiring application within unique cultural and situational contexts)
- *confessional* (derived from the Bible and informed by the creeds, confessions, and teachings of the church)

This thoroughly evangelical approach to theology is presented in a manner that is scaffolded both conceptually and linguistically. Each chapter has a set of paired parables. The first parable of each pair is from a source other than the New Testament, while the second is from Jesus. The first type, those not from the mouth of Jesus, are intended to demonstrate two important things: (1) the popularity of parables in communicating important truths throughout a range of cultures and (2) the various ways that people have

1. Jenefer Philp, Rebecca Adams, and Noriko Iwashita, *Peer Interaction and Second Language Learning* (New York and London: Routledge, 2014).

2. Rod Ellis and Shintani, Natsuko (2014). *Exploring language pedagogy through second language acquisition research.* (Oxford: Routledge, 2014), 158.

addressed issues very similar to those addressed by Jesus. The theological articles appear between the paired parables and are accompanied by a variety of activities. There are two forms of each chapter's article, one being easier and the other more difficult. However, most of the textbook's activities refer directly to the more difficult version, so as students work through each chapter, they will not be able to leave this version unread. Also, while certain readings in the textbook are meant to be read extensively, these articles will need to be read intensively, and perhaps multiple times. With each progressing chapter, the readings, exercises, and tasks place increasing language demands on students. In particular, later chapters (especially 5-7) employ lengthier readings, more complex syntax, and more challenging theological quotations.

The philosophy behind the selection of theological sources used in the development of this textbook is summed up well in the following quote by Kevin Vanhoozer:

> Theology must not hearken to Western voices only. Nor should theologians attend to voices that come only from their century or social class. *All* cultural scenes are equally valid (and equally limited) in the drama of redemption. By contrast, theology should not be anti-Western either. The West has had a considerable head start when thinking about how to apply and contextualize the gospel. . . . Ideally, theologians in one culture will dialogue and learn from theologians in others.[3]

Currently, resources from Western traditions make up the large majority of the world's theological library. In turn, we felt that in order to best prepare students for further theological study, our textbook should reflect this present yet shifting reality. Of course the West does not have the last word on issues of theology. But neither should other traditions claim it either. Rather, this textbook intends to open avenues of dialogue between the many "cultural scenes" that compose the church. Such dialogue reminds us that theological education is never a matter of either giving or taking. Each culture's "validity" and "limitedness" assures us that we all have much to teach to and learn from each other. It is our hope that this textbook will aid students of theology all over the world in joining the church's international dialogue, enabling them not only to listen to it but also to speak into it. Towards this end, as students work through the textbook, they will write their own parable. Through this process, they will creatively communicate theological concepts in ways that directly address their unique cultural and situational contexts. And surely each such context is one that we all need to learn from.[4]

---

3. Kevin Vanhoozer, *The Drama of Doctrine: A Canonical-Linguistic Approach to Christian Theology* (Louisville, KY: Westminster John Knox Press, 2005), 323.

4. For a fuller, and easily accessed, discussion of issues concerning English as a common theological language see Will Bankston, "Global Theology in English: Promising or Problematic?" *The Gospel Coalition*, February 25, 2014, http://thegospelcoalition.org/blogs/tgc/2014/02/25/global-theology-in-english-promising-or-problematic/.

How is the book organized?

Each chapter starts with an overview of the chapter presented in a stand-alone box. Then there is reading material, followed by tasks that allow students to explore the English language as well as the content. Because the book is intended to interest readers (and their teachers) in many different countries, the reading passages go beyond biblical parables. We have included parables or stories of wisdom from a range of countries, including Indonesia, Persia (Iran) and China.

Why focus in each chapter on the form of language, through grammar and vocabulary tasks? After all, this is not basically either a grammar book or one aiming to teach vocabulary. The answer lies in the word awareness. The aim is to make students aware of the forms of language used in theology texts, including the reading and the writing they will be doing.

We also have in mind the multi-level nature of many classes. Our experience tells us that there is no such thing as one-size-fits-all when it comes to textbooks. To try and cater for differences even within one class, we have put together two versions of each theological article, so that students within one class can have the same reading material but be reading at a level that is comfortable for them. We have also supplied more activities than are needed for every class, so that teachers can select and, where necessary, modify the examples.

As far as the order of the chapters is concerned, they are based on topics that students will encounter in their biblical and theological studies. The content in chapters 1-4 is at basically the same level of difficulty. The content in chapters 5-7 is longer and more challenging. Chapter 8 serves as an opportunity for students to review the parable principles and to complete the writing of their own parables.

As authors we have had the privilege of living, working, and organizing workshops for teachers and students in a range of countries. We hope that you enjoy using the book as much as we have enjoyed writing it. We look forward to any feedback that would let us make future editions more useful to teachers and students.

How can you use this textbook?

You can use each chapter of this textbook in the sequence provided. However, you may decide to focus on some chapters and omit others. Each chapter has major sections, each presenting content and exercises that will help your students become more proficient in reading theological materials in English. You can use the text as a supplement to classroom instruction, perhaps using the first four chapters one semester and the final four chapters in the next semester. You may decide to use this text in tutorial sessions or in small groups. Whatever decisions you make as a teacher, we sincerely hope that you will find the readings and exercises helpful in building your students' understanding of theological materials written in English.

Preface for Students

Greetings to our student readers! As we were writing the book we tried to picture the countries where you are living and studying. Are you in Europe or South America, in Asia or in Africa? Perhaps one of us has visited your country.

As you use this book in your class, we hope you can:

- Read the parables with growing understanding
- Apply the parable principles by writing your own parable
- Understand and discuss current theological topics
- Improve your writing in English for study purposes
- Build up your theological vocabulary in English
- Practice taking notes as you listen to presentations and lectures
- Gain confidence in using English with your fellow students

Many of the tasks here have been used by students in different parts of the world. Some people found them easy; others thought they were difficult. With the help of your teacher we hope you will find that your knowledge, skills, and confidence grow chapter by chapter.

1

Sanctification and the Samaritan

Parables are fictional stories that point beyond themselves. They draw their audience into their intriguing narratives, but parables do this to direct them to something deeper. Their most important meaning is not the actual story they tell, but what this story reveals about something else. Parables ultimately refer to and teach about the most important truths of life. Of course, some succeed in giving us wisdom and others do not. Even more, some succeed in revealing the kingdom of God. In this chapter you will focus on two theological concepts: consecration and sanctification. The paired parables will help you explore these two concepts.

PART I: An Indonesian Parable

Before Reading Consider…

- What does holiness mean?
- What does a holy person look like?
- How does someone become holy?

The Farmer and the Holy Man

(1) An Indonesian farmer was returning to his village when he suddenly stopped on the jungle trail and stared ahead with growing alarm. Lying across his path he could see a tiger's tail and looking carefully, he could see that that tail belonged to a very large and very fierce tiger. This tiger was waiting for him. Acting on impulse the farmer put down his scythe, ran forward and seized the beast by the tail. With an angry snarl the tiger tried to free his tail, but the more he roared and plunged, the harder the farmer held on.

(2) The struggle went on for a while, and then, just as the farmer felt he could hang on no longer, who should come along the path but an Indonesian holy man? The holy man stopped, surveyed the scene with interest and was about to pass on when the farmer called to him.

(3) "Dear holy man," he cried, "please take my scythe and kill this tiger. I can't hold on much longer."

(4) The holy man sighed. "My friend," he replied, "that I cannot do. I am forbidden by the rites of my religion to kill any living thing."

(5) The farmer renewed his failing grip. "But holy man, don't you see that if you fail to kill this tiger then it will kill me. Surely the life of a man is more valuable than the life of a beast!"

(6) The holy man folded his arms in the depths of his flowing robe. "About that, I cannot speak. All around me in the jungle I see things killing and being killed. I am not responsible for these things; neither can I help them. But for me to kill…ah, this I cannot do."

(7) Just then the tiger gave a vicious snarl and a furious pull on his tail. Sweat poured from the farmer. The holy man prepared to leave. "Dear holy man," sobbed the farmer in despair, "don't go! If it is against the rules of your faith to kill the beast, at least come and hold its tail while I kill him."

(8) The holy man paused and considered. "I suppose I could do that," he conceded at last. "There can be no harm in holding the animal's tail." Cautiously he approached the infuriated best and joined the farmer in holding his tail. "Do you have him, holy man?" panted the farmer. "Do you have him fast?"

(9) "Yes, yes," said the holy man, "but hurry before he gets loose." In a leisurely manner the farmer brushed off his clothes. Slowly he picked up his scythe and prepared to leave.

(10) "Here, where are you going?" demanded the holy man. "I thought you were going to kill the tiger."

(11) The farmer folded his arms in the sleeve of his coat and sighed. "Dear holy man," he replied, "you are a most excellent teacher. You have completely converted me to your most noble religion. I can see how wrong I have been all these years. I cannot kill this tiger, for it is against the rules of your holy religion. As you taught me, all around us in the jungle we see things killing and being killed. We are not responsible for these things, but for us holy men to kill, as you say, this cannot be. I am going into the village yonder, so you will have to hold on to this tiger until some other man comes along not so motivated by the high ideals of our holy faith. Perhaps you will come to convert him too, as you converted me." And with this parting shot, the farmer left.

Notes/Questions

Think-Pair-Share

1) Summarize the teaching of the parable in one sentence.

2) What does this parable teach about the values and beliefs of the culture it came from?

3) What is a well-known parable or other type of story from your culture? What does it teach? Tell the story to your classmates.

➲ Reading Strategy: Put These In Order[1]

Using numbers 1-16, put the statements in the right order. The parable is divided into two parts. Compare your answers with a partner.

1) Use numbers 1-8

_____ A holy man came along.

_____ The farmer saw the tiger's tail on the path.

_____ The holy man said he could not kill the tiger.

_____ The farmer quickly took hold of the tail and held on.

_____ An Indonesian farmer was on his way home.

_____ The farmer begged him to kill the tiger with his scythe.

_____ The farmer put down his scythe.

_____ The tiger struggled to get loose.

2) Use numbers 9-15

_____ The farmer picked up his scythe and started to leave.

_____ The holy man thought there was no harm in holding the tiger's tail.

_____ The farmer was wet with sweat.

_____ The holy man was holding on to the tiger's tail.

_____ The farmer explained that he had been converted to the holy man's religion.

_____ The farmer wanted the holy man to hold on to the tiger's tail so that he could kill the beast.

_____ The holy man would have to hold on to the tiger's tail until someone else came along to help.

1. For this section, you can check your work with the Answer Key found in the back of this book.

Vocabulary Focus[2]

Match the numbered words with the lettered words that seem to have about the same or nearly the same meaning in the story.

Example

1. __a__ trail — a. path

1)	______	snarl	a) carefully	j) classic
2)	______	rite	b) stopped	k) roar
3)	______	faith	c) angry	l) fierce
4)	______	cautiously	d) change	
5)	______	vicious	e) surveyed	
6)	______	considered	f) religion	
7)	______	paused	g) thought	
8)	______	convert	h) tale	
9)	______	furious	i) religious act	

Theological Connection

1) Describe the attitudes and actions of the holy man in the story.

____

____

____

2) Does this description agree or disagree with your own conception of a holy man? Why?

____

____

____

3) In Romans 2:3, Paul asks a "hypothetical dialogue partner,"[3] "Do you suppose, O man—you who judge those who practice such things and yet do them yourself—

---

2. For this section, you can check your work with the Answer Key found in the back of this book.

3. Colin G. Kruse, *Paul's Letter to the Romans. The Pillar New Testament Commentary* Series, ed. D.A. Carson (Grand Rapids, MI: Eerdmans, 2012), 119.

that you will escape the judgment of God?" How do Paul's words relate to the actions of the holy man in the parable?

____

____

____

PART II: Furthering Your Knowledge

Keeping in mind your conception of a holy man, read the following passage about holiness. Read the left column if you want something more difficult or the right column for something easier.

As you read, underline parts you would like to ask questions about. Use the lines at the end of this reading to write down any questions you might have for your teacher.

Consecration and Sanctification

Difficult	Simplified
(1) Albert Wolters makes a distinction between the theological terms *consecration* and *sanctification*, which both mean to make holy.[4] Their difference lies in how something is made holy. To consecrate is "...to set apart, to dedicate, to devote to the service or worship of God."[5] To sanctify, however, is "... to make free from sin, to cleanse from moral corruption, to purify."[6] These terms describe different ways of relating to God's creation, which includes the whole world and everything in it.	(1) Albert Wolters says there are two words that mean to make holy. The words *consecration* and *sanctification* answer the question, how is something made holy?[4] *Consecration* means "...to set apart, to dedicate, to devote to the service or worship of God."[5] The second word, *sanctification*, means "...to make free from sin, to cleanse from moral corruption, to purify."[6] These words are important for our relationship with God's creation: the whole world and everything in it.

4. Albert Wolters, *Creation Regained: Biblical Basics for a Reformational Woldview, 2nd Edition* (Grand Rapids, MI: Eerdmans, 2005), 89.

5. Ibid.

6. Ibid.

(2) Ever since Adam and Eve disobeyed God, every part of our world has been polluted by sin. Although all of it was once pure, nothing is now free from sin's corruption.[7] In response, we must ask ourselves how the world can be cleansed of its sin.

(2) Ever since Adam and Eve disobeyed God, every part of our world has been made dirty by sin. Although the whole world was once pure, nothing is now free from sin's harm.[7] Our question is this: How can the world be cleansed of its sin?

(3) When we apply the terms of consecration and sanctification to this question of cleansing, they give us very different answers. If we think of sin as a sickness, consecration urges us to quarantine the infected parts of creation, separating the sick from the healthy. In contrast, sanctification seeks to cure, not quarantine. Like a pill that someone swallows, sanctification starts healing the person from the inside and then works outward, eventually curing the whole body.

(3) Let's look again at the two words: consecration and sanctification. These give us two different answers. Sin is like an illness. For some infectious illnesses we have to go away from other people. We call that quarantine. That's like consecration. But sanctification is like medicine or a pill. When we swallow a pill our bodies start to heal from the inside towards the outside. Finally, the whole body is well.

(4) Since all of creation is infected with sin, consecration through quarantining cannot purge the pollution of sin. There can be no separation of the healthy from the unhealthy because everything is sick. However, the Holy Spirit enables us to undertake the process of purging our sin. This cleansing work of the Spirit in us is the foundational reality of sanctification, but we can apply this process of sanctification to all of creation. By the working of the Holy Spirit in us, we must also work to sanctify our families, our communities, our companies, our countries, and so on. Of course, in this life, sanctification will never be complete, but anything being sanctified is always becoming healthier, purer, and freer from the corruption of sin.

(4) Because all of creation has an infection, creation cannot be made better by quarantining. We cannot separate the healthy things from unhealthy things, because everything is sick. However, the Holy Spirit enables us to undertake the process of purging our sin. This process is our sanctification and, through the Holy Spirit, we can also work to make all of creation holy. No part of creation is free from this need. With the help of the Holy Spirit, we must also work to sanctify our families, communities, companies, countries, and so on. Of course, in this life, sanctification is never finished, but anything being sanctified is always becoming healthier, purer, and freer from the sickness of sin.

7. Romans 8:20-21.

(5) However, consecration is not an invalid process. Instead, like any process, it becomes troublesome when it is applied in the wrong way. In the Old Testament, certain objects were consecrated for the service of the temple and, even now, consecration is important in the life of the church, carried out in activities such as the administration of the sacraments. Dangers come when one biblical theme is pushed too far to the exclusion of others. We need to keep this in mind when examining the relationship between consecration and sanctification. Even the church itself is to be in the world but not of the world, which implies a kind of simultaneous sanctification and consecration. There is a complexity here that we must not oversimplify, especially as we consider Christian worship.

(6) However, Wolters points out that the Old Testament predicted a more perfect system of worship, one in which even the most common household objects would become tools of worship. As Wolters quotes from the book of Zechariah, "On that day 'Holy to the Lord' will be inscribed on the bells of horses… Every pot in Jerusalem and Judah will be holy to the Lord almighty (14:20-21)."[8] Similarly, the tools we daily work with, whether books or bricks, can likewise be used to worship God when they become tools for sanctifying the world around us. When this happens, the Holy Spirit is using us to make the world a holier place.

(5) However, consecration is also an important process. Like any process, consecration can be a problem if it is done in the wrong way. In the Old Testament, special objects were consecrated for the temple. And still today the church uses consecration in important activities such as the sacraments. It is dangerous to only focus on one biblical theme and forget the others. This truth is important when we think about the relationship between consecration and sanctification. Even the church itself is to be in the world but not of the world, which implies both sanctification and consecration. There is a complex connection between sanctification and consecration that we cannot oversimplify, especially when we worship God.

(6) However, Wolters points out that the Old Testament looked ahead to a more perfect system of worship, where even the most common household objects would become tools of worship. As Wolters quotes from the book of Zechariah, "On that day 'Holy to the Lord' will be inscribed on the bells of horses… Every pot in Jerusalem and Judah will be holy to the Lord almighty (14:20-21)."[8] In the same way, the tools we work with every day, whether books or bricks, can also be used to praise God when they become tools for sanctifying the world around us. When this happens the Holy Spirit uses us to make the world a holier place.

8. Wolters, *Creation Regained*, 90.

Notes/Questions

____

____

____

____

____

____

____

Vocabulary Focus[9]

Here are some parts from the reading again. In the left hand column there are spaces to fill in. To make the exercise more difficult, cover the right hand column. For more help, look at the right hand column, where the nine words are put in alphabetical order.

Fill in the missing words	*Find the words here*
1) Two words mean "to make holy." The words are __________ and __________.	*cleansed* *consecration* *creation* *devote* *infectious* *pure* *sanctification* *sanctified* *sanctify*
2) One word means to __________ ourselves to the service or worship of God.	
3) The second word means to make the person __________.	
4) The two words are important for people and for all __________.	
5) How can the world be __________ of its sin?	
6) For some __________ illnesses we have to go away from other people.	
7) With the help of the Holy Spirit, we work to __________ our families and our communities.	
8) As things are __________ they will be consecrated because they will stand out from others like them.	

9. For this section, you can check your work with the Answer Key found in the back of this book.

Think More About the Meaning

1) After reading this passage, how has your understanding of holiness changed?

2) Is the holy man's concept of holiness more similar to consecration or sanctification? Why?

3) Would the farmer from the parable find consecration or sanctification more important to his situation? Why?

4) How could the holy man have worked to sanctify the situation presented in the parable?

PART III: A Parable of Jesus

Before Reading Consider…

Sanctification and Justification

One theological danger is to confuse *sanctification* and *justification*. Louis Berkhof supplies us a firm foundation in distinguishing these two terms. He defines sanctification as

"...that gracious and continuous operation of the Holy Spirit, by which he delivers the justified sinner from the pollution of sin, renews his whole nature in the image of God, and enables him to perform good works."[10] Take a moment and paraphrase each part of the three-part process that Berkhof describes:

1) ______________________________

____

____

____

2) ______________________________

____

____

____

3) ______________________________

____

____

____

Like Wolters, Berkhof describes sanctification as the cleansing from "the pollution of sin." He says that it is "the justified sinner" who is delivered from sin in this process. That is, the sinner is first justified and then begins the process of sanctification. Justification is the legal verdict by which God forgives our sins and declares us to be righteous, all on the basis of Christ's perfect fulfillment of God's law. Therefore, sanctification transforms us to match the verdict that God has already and irrevocably given that we are justified.

However, if we affirm sanctification without justification, we will rely on our own righteousness rather than the righteousness of Christ for this verdict. This is called *legalism*. We will constantly wonder if we have been good enough to satisfy God's standard. Of course, God's standard is complete perfection and we can never meet it. Only Christ can. On the other hand, if we affirm justification without sanctification, we will not seek to be conformed to the perfect righteousness of Christ. This is called *antinomianism*.

10. Louis Berkhof, *Systematic Theology, Combined Edition* (Grand Rapids, MI: Eerdmans, 1996), 532.

We will believe that since Christ has already met God's standard for us, it then makes no difference if we go on sinning or not. In the end, both errors ridicule the person and work of Christ: legalism through pride in one's own ability and antinomianism through love of self rather than love of God.

Strategy: Venn Diagram

With these things in mind, use the Venn diagram below to compare and contrast justification and sanctification.

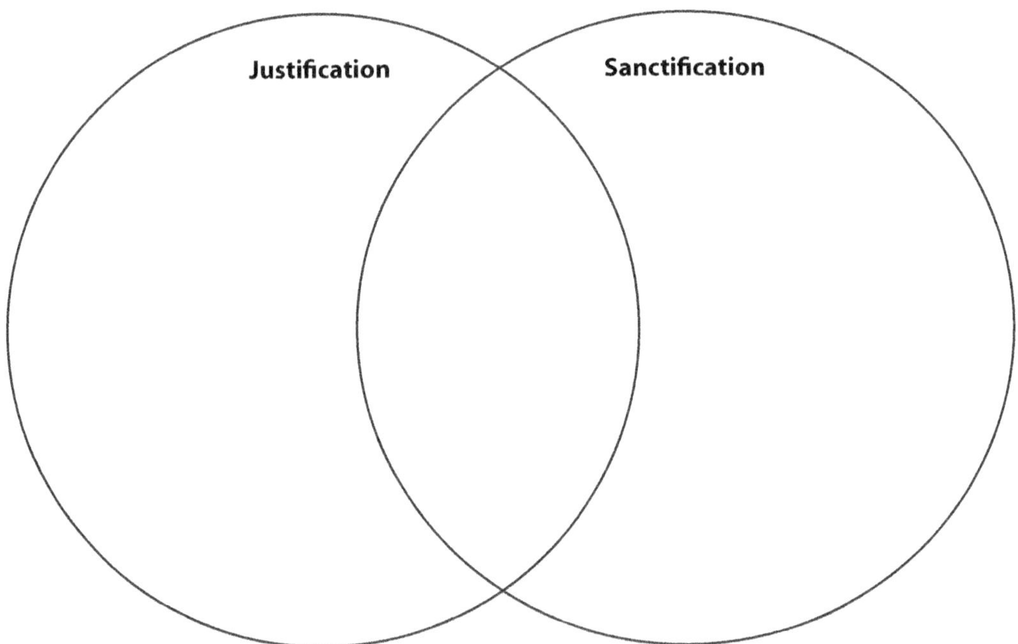

Man's Desire for Justification

Jesus tells the following parable in response to a question that a man asked because he was "desiring to justify himself." This is a desire that tempts all of us and it relates to the error of legalism described above. Why do you think we naturally desire to justify ourselves and why does Jesus oppose this desire?

____

____

____

____

The Parable of the Good Samaritan

And behold, a lawyer stood up to put him to the test, saying, "Teacher, what shall I do to inherit eternal life?" He said to him, "What is written in the Law? How do you read it?" And he answered, "You shall love the Lord your God with all your heart and with all your soul and with all your strength and with all your mind, and your neighbor as yourself." And he said to him, "You have answered correctly; do this, and you will live."

But he, desiring to justify himself, said to Jesus, "And who is my neighbor?" Jesus replied, "A man was going down from Jerusalem to Jericho, and he fell among robbers, who stripped him and beat him and departed, leaving him half dead. Now by chance a priest was going down that road, and when he saw him he passed by on the other side. So likewise a Levite, when he came to the place and saw him, passed by on the other side. But a Samaritan, as he journeyed, came to where he was, and when he saw him, he had compassion. He went to him and bound up his wounds, pouring on oil and wine. Then he set him on his own animal and brought him to an inn and took care of him. And the next day he took out two denarii and gave them to the innkeeper, saying, 'Take care of him, and whatever more you spend, I will repay you when I come back.' Which of these three, do you think, proved to be a neighbor to the man who fell among the robbers?" He said, "The one who showed him mercy." And Jesus said to him, "You go, and do likewise."

(Luke 10:25-37)

Important Cultural Information

- The Jews and the Samaritans disliked each other very much. John 4:9 tells us that these two people groups had "no dealings" with each other.
- It is significant that all of the travelers are going from Jerusalem to Jericho. For the Priest and the Levite, this implies that they have just finished a *consecrated* form of worship at the temple and are now returning home.

Key Issues

1) Why does the lawyer ask Jesus the first question?

____

____

____

____

2) How does the lawyer wrongly try to use the term "neighbor" as a tool for consecration? What distinction between people is he trying to make?

3) According to Jesus, who is our neighbor? How does he see "neighbor" as a term of inclusion rather than exclusion?

4) How did the priest and the Levite miss an opportunity to worship God after they worshipped at the temple in Jerusalem?

Personal Reflection

Jesus surprised his Jewish audience by telling a parable in which a person from a group they disliked actually saved the life of a Jew.

1) How might Jesus have told this story in your culture or another culture you know about? What kind of person would be the traveler and what kind of person would be the Samaritan?

2) Now imagine Jesus telling this revised parable to an audience made of people who are of the same group as you made the traveler. What do you think the audience's response would be?

____

____

____

____

The Love that Fulfills the Law

In rightly summarizing the Law, the lawyer states, "You shall love the Lord your God with all your heart and with all your soul and with all your strength and with all your mind, and your neighbor as yourself." Compare this line with the following excerpt from the passage about holiness. It reads, "Like a pill that someone swallows, sanctification starts healing the person from the inside and then works outward, eventually curing the whole body."

1) Regarding sanctification, who might we consider "the pill" that heals us inwardly?

____

____

____

____

2) As described by the lawyer, what is the first and most important step in our inward healing? That is, whom should we love first and how?

____

____

____

____

3) After this first step of healing, what is the next step? That is, whom should we love next and how? How is this second step demonstrated outwardly in Jesus' parable?

____

____

____

____

Loving God and the process of sanctification are directly related. As Michael Reeves writes, "The Father has eternally known and loved his great Son, and through the Spirit he opens our eyes that we too might know him, and so he wins our hearts that we too might love him."[11] The Spirit enables us to love Christ and this love makes us more and more like Christ. This is because worship transforms us. As we worship someone or something, we become more and more like our object of worship. And we worship what we love and desire most. Therefore, as the Spirit gives us greater love and desire for Christ, the Spirit is sanctifying us because he is making us more like Christ.

4) With this in mind, think about the lawyer's summary of the law. How does the love of Christ, which makes us more like Christ, lead us to love our neighbor as ourselves?

____

____

____

____

What tools does the Samaritan use to sanctify the world around him and how does he use them?	What tools can you use to sanctify the world around you and how can you use them?
1) He uses oil and wine, pouring them onto the traveler's wounds	1) I can use my theological education to…
2)	2)
3)	3)

11. Michael Reeves, *Delighting in the Trinity: An Introduction to the Christian Faith* (Downers Grove, IL: InterVarsity, 2012), 94.

Making Connections

1) Take a few minutes and make some notes comparing and contrasting the Indonesian parable and Jesus' parable. For example, consider the parables' characters, situations, and meanings.

Similarities between the two parables	Things unique to the Indonesian parable	Things unique to Jesus' parable

2) In his famous address, *The Weight of Glory,* C.S. Lewis says, "Next to the Blessed Sacrament itself, your neighbor is the holiest object presented to your senses."[12] Write this statement in your own words.

____

____

____

____

12. C.S. Lewis, "The Weight of Glory" in *The Weight of Glory and Other Addresses* (New York, NY: Touchstone, 1996), 40.

3) Think of all the characters in the two parables and decide if each would agree or disagree with the wisdom of this statement.

Who would agree?	Who would disagree?

PART IV: Writing Your Own Parable

Parable Principle 1
Jesus' parables are concise, to the point, and have a very important purpose. They were not just stories to entertain his audience. He told them to change the beliefs, attitudes, and behaviors of his listeners.

1) What beliefs, attitudes, and behaviors does the parable of the good Samaritan intend to change?

____

____

____

____

2) How does your answer to the previous question relate to the ways that the Indonesian parable seeks to change its audience?

____

____

____

____

Think about beliefs, behaviors, and attitudes that you would like to see change so that they reflect the gospel of Jesus Christ. Think about the ways that sin has infected situations that you daily encounter. The parable you write will aim to help sanctify these situations. For instance, consider common beliefs, attitudes, and actions towards God, the church, salvation, the poor, the sick, other cultures, or the environment (to name only a few possibilities) which conflict with the person and work of Christ. Then choose a specific example, but make sure it is personally meaningful to you because you will return to it in each chapter as you create your own parable. Describe your example below.

2

Communicating the Kingdom

In this chapter you will encounter two of the textbook's more complex parables. When reading these parables, you will examine how they communicate two levels of meaning. The first level is often easy to understand, but it takes an observant audience to understand their deeper meaning. In particular, you will investigate how Jesus' parables reveal the kingdom of God.

PART I: A Parable from Charles Spurgeon (United Kingdom)

Before Reading Consider...

- Who was a famous ruler of your country in the past?
- How did people show respect to that ruler?
- Were there special gifts people gave that ruler?

The King, Gardener, and Nobleman

(1) Once upon a time there was a king who ruled over everything in his land. One day there was a gardener who grew an enormous carrot. He took it to his king and said, "My lord, this is the greatest carrot I've ever grown or ever will grow; therefore, I want to present it to you as a token of my love and respect for you."

(2) The king was touched and discerned the man's heart, so as he turned to go, the king said, "Wait! You are clearly a good steward of the earth. I want to give a plot of land to you freely as a gift, so you can garden it all." The gardener was amazed and delighted and went home rejoicing. But there was a nobleman at the king's court who overheard all this, and he said, "My! If that is what you get for a carrot, what if you gave the king something better?"

(3) The next day the nobleman came before the king, and he was leading a handsome black stallion. He bowed low and said, "My lord, I breed horses, and this is the greatest horse I've ever bred or ever will; therefore, I want to present it to you as a token of my love and respect for you."

(4) But the king discerned his heart and said, "Thank you," and took the horse and simply dismissed him. The nobleman was perplexed, so the king said, "Let me explain. That gardener was giving me the carrot, but you were giving yourself the horse."

Notes/Questions

____

____

____

____

____

Vocabulary Focus[1]

Locate each boldfaced word in the parable. Circle the word. Look up the word in your English dictionary. Write the part of speech the word belongs to and a short definition that is appropriate for the word.

Example

enormous: There was a gardener who grew an **enormous** carrot.

adjective — very large in size

(part of speech) (definition)

1) **token:** I want to present it to you as a **token** of my love and respect for you.

__________ ______________________________

(part of speech) (definition)

2) **discerned:** But the king **discerned** his heart.

__________ ______________________________

(part of speech) (definition)

1. For this section, you can check your work with the Answer Key found in the back of this book.

3) **plot:** I want to give a **plot** of land to you freely as a gift.

__________ ____________________________________

(part of speech) (definition)

4) **overheard:** There was a nobleman in the court who **overhead** all of this.

__________ ____________________________________

(part of speech) (definition)

5) **dismissed:** The king took the horse and simply **dismissed** him.

__________ ____________________________________

(part of speech) (definition)

6) **perplexed:** The nobleman was **perplexed** so the king said, "Let me explain."

__________ ____________________________________

(part of speech) (definition)

7) **breed (bred):** "My lord, I **breed** horses and this is the greatest horse I've ever **bred**."

__________ ____________________________________

(part of speech) (definition)

8) **steward:** You are clearly a good **steward** of the earth.

__________ ____________________________________

(part of speech) (definition)

9) **simply:** He **simply** dismissed him.

__________ ____________________________________

(part of speech) (definition)

10) **better:** What if you gave the king something **better**?

__________ ____________________________________

(part of speech) (definition)

Think-Pair-Share

First, use the diagram below to explain to a partner the relationships between each character in the parable.

Example

The nobleman is wealthier than the gardener and has a better gift to offer to the king.

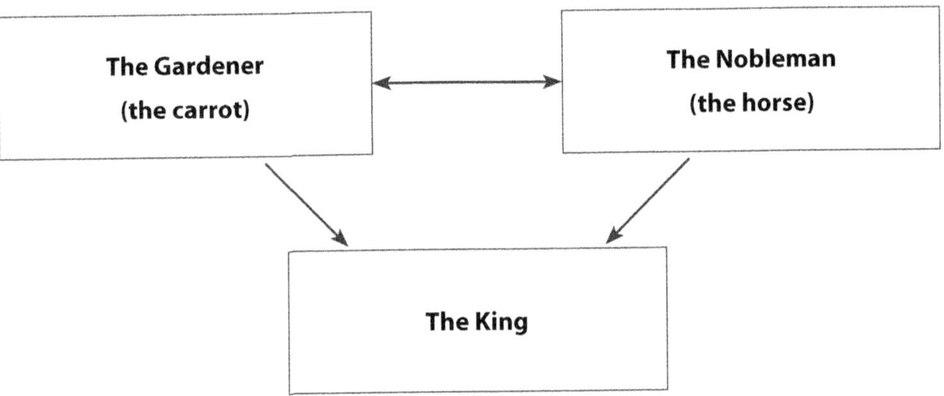

Next, make up some interview questions about the parable. Some questions could have more than one right answer.

Work in groups to make up the questions. Then each person finds someone from another group to interview. You should have six questions each starting with a different word:

1) Who…
2) What…
3) Where…
4) When…
5) Why…
6) Which…

Theological Connection

1) Why did the gardener give the king the carrot? How does this purpose honor the king?

____

____

____

____

2) How might the gardener have felt if the king had only thanked him and not given him the plot of land?

____

____

____

____

3) Did the nobleman love the king or the things the king could give him? How do you know?

____

____

____

____

4) Imagine other good stewards that love and respect the king. What gifts could they give the king? Complete the chart below using common professions from your culture. An example is provided below.

Profession	Gift
Teacher	After much research and preparation, a teacher could present a lesson to the king on a subject that the king finds interesting.

PART II: Furthering Your Knowledge

Keeping in mind the joy of the gardener, read the following passage about glorifying Christ the king by enjoying him. Read the left column if you want something more difficult or the right column for something easier.

As you read, underline parts you would like to ask questions about. Use the lines at the end of this reading to write down any questions you might have for your teacher.

Enjoyment & the Kingdom of God

Difficult	Simplified
(1) *The Westminster Shorter Catechism* states, "Man's chief end is to glorify God, and to enjoy him forever." This is an essential truth, stressing that only in God can we find the true purpose of our lives. However, John Piper points out that the conjunction "and" can be unclear. He affirms that the theologians who composed this statement believed that both glorifying God and enjoying God constituted the same "end." If they hadn't, they would have instead written that these two activities were man's chief ends. However, the "and" might lead some people to separate these two actions. They might think that at certain times you give him glory and, at other times, he gives you enjoyment.[2]	(1) *The Westminster Shorter Catechism* says, "Man's chief end is to glorify God, and to enjoy him forever." This true saying means that we find our true purpose only in God. However, John Piper says that the word "and" can be unclear. The people who wrote the catechism said that bringing glory to God and enjoying God constitute the same end. If they were different the word "end" would be "ends". Of course "and" can join two separate things. Then the meaning would be that sometimes we give him glory and, at other times, he gives us joy.[2]

2. John Piper, *Desiring God: Meditations of a Christian Hedonist* (Portland, OR: Multnomah, 2003), 17.

(2) In turn, Piper reworks this statement, omitting the conjunction and adding a gerund for manner. He writes, "The chief end of man is to glorify God by enjoying Him forever."[3] Gerunds for manner explain how to do something and Piper explains that we best glorify God by enjoying him. Towards this end, he declares, "God is most glorified in me when I am most satisfied in Him."[4]

(2) Piper has rewritten the sentence to say, "The chief end of man is to glorify God by enjoying him forever."[3] In other words, Piper's sentence tells us how we best give God glory. We do this by enjoying him. As Piper writes, "God is most glorified in me when I am most satisfied in him."[4]

(3) So then, this present life, while certainly full of suffering, is also full of joy. We have joy because we have fellowship with God and enjoying this glorifies God. Of course, our fellowship in the present age is not yet perfect. Our sin still hinders it and limits our enjoyment of God. Even still, the possibility of such fellowship, despite its present imperfection, means something very important. It means the next age has begun breaking into our current age.

(3) This means that in our life right now we do have suffering, but we also have joy. Why? Because we are a part of God's family. Being a part of God's family brings glory to God. Of course, our fellowship here and now is still not perfect. Our sin still comes in the way of our fellowship with God and makes us enjoy him less. Even so, being able to have this less-than-perfect fellowship is something very important. It means the next age has begun coming into our present time.

(4) When we speak of the next age, we mean the age that will begin with the second coming of Christ. On that day Jesus will be acknowledged by all of creation as the king of the universe. Our enjoyment of him will then be full. However, because we are able to enjoy him in the present age, his kingship and kingdom must also be a present reality. That is, he is already our king, and we are already his people.

(4) When we say the next age, we mean the age that will begin with the second coming of Christ. On that day all creation will acknowledge Jesus as the king of the universe. Our joy in him will then be full. However, because we are able to enjoy him now, Christ's kingship and his kingdom are true now. That is, he is already our king, and we are already his people.

3. Ibid., 18.

4. Ibid., 10.

(5) Jesus illustrates this tension in his frequent teachings on the kingdom of God. For instance, he tells his disciples, "...for behold, the kingdom of God is in the midst of you,"[5] but, on another occasion he says, "I will not drink again of the fruit of the vine until that day when I drink it new in the kingdom of God."[6] In the first passage the kingdom of God has already arrived, but in the second, it has not yet come. In turn, Jesus shows that the kingdom of God is, as many theologians have put it, "already but not yet." However, even when the next age begins and the kingdom of God has fully arrived, our chief end will not change. It remains the same "forever." We will still glorify him by enjoying him, but much more fully than we do now.	(5) Jesus often explained what these words mean in his teachings on the kingdom of God. Once he told his disciples, "...for behold, the kingdom of God is in the midst of you,"[5] but, another time he said, "I will not drink again of the fruit of the vine until that day when I drink it new in the kingdom of God."[6] In the first passage the kingdom of God has already arrived, but in the second, it has not yet come. Jesus shows two things. First, the kingdom of God is, as many people have put it, "already but not yet." However, even when the next age begins and the kingdom of God has fully arrived, our chief goal will not change. It remains the same "forever." We will still glorify him by enjoying him, but much more fully than we do now.

Notes/Questions

____

____

____

____

Grammar Focus[7]

Use the examples of a gerund and an infinitive below to complete the following exercise:

Gerund: Verb + gerund	verb + gerund I enjoy <u>reading</u> the Bible.
Infinitive: Verb + infinitive	verb + infinitive We've decided <u>to read</u> the Bible daily.

5. Luke 17:21.

6. Mark 14:25.

7. For this section, you can check your work with the Answer Key found in the back of this book.

Read the following sentences. Circle the verb and underline the gerund(s) or infinitive(s) in each sentence. Decide if the underlined words are gerunds or infinitives. Write the correct answer in the blank(s) on the right.

Example
I (started) studying for the exam on Tuesday. gerund

1) The *Westminster Shorter Catechism* states that, "Man's chief end is to glorify God and to enjoy him forever." __________

2) We enjoy glorifying him in our daily work. __________

3) We are called to glorify him in the present age. __________

4) It means the next age has begun breaking into our current age. __________

5) He finished reading the *Westminster Shorter Catechism* at midnight. __________

6) He prepared to go to the church and to preach his sermon. __________

Think More About the Meaning

1) How does the statement in paragraph 2, "The chief end of man is to glorify God by enjoying Him forever," relate to the actions of the gardener?

____

____

____

____

2) How can we, like the gardener, focus on enjoying God more than the things he can give us?

____

____

____

____

3) What does the article mean when it says the kingdom of God is "already but not yet"?

___

___

___

___

4) Think about your answers for the chart you completed for question 4 in the previous section. How could someone give each of these gifts to God (like the gardener) rather than to himself (like the nobleman)? It might be helpful to refer to the sections in chapter 1 about *sanctification* and the parable of the good Samaritan. Write your answers in the chart below. An example is provided. Discuss your answers with a partner.

Gift from previous chart	How can this gift be given to God?
Interesting lesson	We can teach others about the world that God created through academic subjects, helping them to more fully understand and enjoy his creation.

PART III: A Parable of Jesus

Before Reading Consider…

1) What does the word *shrewd* mean?
2) Who are some shrewd people from the Bible?
3) What are some characteristics of a shrewd manager?

The Parable of the Dishonest Manager

He also said to the disciples, "There was a rich man who had a manager, and charges were brought to him that this man was wasting his possessions. And he called him and said to him, 'What is this that I hear about you? Turn in the account of your management, for you can no longer be manager.' And the manager said to himself, 'What shall I do, since my master is taking the management away from me? I am not strong enough to dig, and I am ashamed to beg. I have decided what to do, so that when I am removed from management, people may receive me into their houses.' So, summoning his master's debtors one by one, he said to the first, 'How much do you owe my master?' He said, 'A hundred measures of oil.' He said to him, 'Take your bill, and sit down quickly and write fifty.' Then he said to another, 'And how much do you owe?' He said, 'A hundred measures of wheat.' He said to him, 'Take your bill, and write eighty.' The master commended the dishonest manager for his shrewdness. For the sons of this world are more shrewd in dealing with their own generation than the sons of light. And I tell you, make friends for yourselves by means of unrighteous wealth, so that when it fails they may receive you into the eternal dwellings.

"One who is faithful in a very little is also faithful in much, and one who is dishonest in a very little is also dishonest in much. If then you have not been faithful in the unrighteous wealth, who will entrust to you the true riches? And if you have not been faithful in that which is another's, who will give you that which is your own? No servant can serve two masters, for either he will hate the one and love the other, or he will be devoted to the one and despise the other. You cannot serve God and money."

The Pharisees, who were lovers of money, heard all these things, and they ridiculed him. And he said to them, "You are those who justify yourselves before men, but God knows your hearts. For what is exalted among men is an abomination in the sight of God."

(Luke 16:1-15)

➡ Important Cultural Information

- A manager, like the one described, would be the full representative of his master. If he made an agreement, it was the same as if his master had made it.[8]
- The term translated here as "unrighteous wealth" was a common phrase for "all money" and it did not imply that it was money acquired through bad or evil means.[9]

8. Klyne Snodgrass, *Stories with Intent: A Comprehensive Guide to the Parables of Jesus* (Grand Rapids, MI: Eerdmans, 2008), 406.

9. Craig L. Blomberg, *Interpreting the Parables* (Downers Grove, IL:InterVarsity, 1990), 246.

Personal Reflection

1) This is often considered the most difficult parable of Jesus to interpret. Why do you think this is so?

2) How did the manager act shrewdly? Does this make him more like the gardener or the nobleman in Spurgeon's parable?

3) Who was the true master of the manager, the rich man or the rich man's money?

This World and the Kingdom of God

In this parable, Jesus is contrasting this world we live in with the kingdom of God. Jesus says, "...the sons of this world are more shrewd in dealing with their own generation than the sons of light." The manager acted boldly according to the norms of this world. However, the sons of light do not act as boldly according to norms of the kingdom of God. The manager's actions were wicked, but they gave him a temporary dwelling place in a wicked world. Our actions, as sons of light, should be good and will prepare us for an eternal dwelling place when the kingdom of God fully arrives. As John Piper writes, "The aim of this parable is to instruct the disciples in the right and loving use of worldly possessions... In other words, don't care about earthly reward; look to the heavenly reward – namely, the infinite joys of being a son of God!"[10]

10. Piper, *Desiring God*, 194-195.

1) Did the manager use his resources "rightly and lovingly?" What reward did he seek?

____

____

____

____

2) The parable is not saying that money is a bad thing, but that it becomes a bad thing when it is our king instead of Jesus. How can we use money "rightly and lovingly" so that it demonstrates Jesus' kingship?

____

____

____

Grammar Focus[11]

Organizational markers help you to understand how the story is organized and how to identify the key points in the story. Terms like *first, second, therefore,* and *in conclusion* are examples of organizational markers.

Directions: Read the following paragraph and circle the three organizational markers that end in *–ly*. Write them in the chart on the following page. Next, include on the chart the realm that comes after each organizational marker. Also include a Bible reference that is an example of that specific realm.

Realms of the Kingdom[12]

The theologian Geerhardus Vos asserted that the kingdom of God is not just in our hearts, but also around us, working to defeat all of the evil present in this world. In particular, he identified three main aspects of the kingdom, which give us a fuller understanding of its character and purpose. Firstly, it is the realm of God's saving grace in which people are saved by God's grace and not their own works. Secondly, it is the realm of righteousness and justice in which people live according to new rules of conduct. And thirdly, it is the realm of God's blessing and joy in which God's people currently enjoy God and his redeeming of creation, though not yet in full.[13]

---

11. For this section, you can check your work with the Answer Key found in the back of this book.

12. A *realm* is an area of knowledge, interest, or activity such as new discoveries in the realm of medicine. It can also mean a country or place ruled by a king or queen.

13. Timothy Keller, *Center Church: Doing Balanced Gospel Ministry in Your City* (Grand Rapids, MI: Zondervan, 2012), 229. In this section, Keller summarizes Vos' *The Teaching of Jesus Concerning the Kingdom of God.*

Organizational Marker 1	Organizational Marker 2	Organizational Marker 3
Realm of	Realm of	Realm of
Bible reference	Bible reference	Bible reference

The three organizational markers begin sentences that describe three aspects about the kingdom of God. Since we are citizens of this kingdom, each of these aspects affects our lives. Fill in the chart below, explaining how each realm affects your daily life.

Realm of Kingdom of God	Effect on your daily life
The Realm of God's Saving Grace	
The Realm of God's Righteousness and Justice	
The Realm of God's Blessing and Joy	

Making Connections: Conduct in the Kingdom of God

Jesus says, "For what is exalted among men is an abomination in the sight of God." This makes a strong distinction between this world and the kingdom of God.

Find a passage in the gospels in which Jesus demonstrates or explains the proper conduct of the kingdom of God. First cite the passage and then paraphrase it and show how it connects to the Kingdom of God. An example has been provided.

Example

Passage: Luke 9:46-48

Paraphrase:

> While the disciples were arguing about which of them was the greatest, Jesus placed a child beside him, which was a position of honor.[14] In the Kingdom of God, the person who is the greatest is the one who welcomes and serves everyone else, including children, which was a group not highly honored in that society.

Passage:

Paraphrase:

____

____

____

____

Now find a passage in which the Pharisees show the usual actions of the kingdom of this world. First cite the passage and then paraphrase it and show how it "...is an abomination in the sight of God" and how it is similar to the actions of the nobleman in Spurgeon's parable.

Passage:

Paraphrase:

____

____

____

____

14. Joel B. Green, *The Gospel of Luke, New International Commentary on the New Testament* Series, ed. Gordon Fee (Grand Rapids, MI: Eerdmans, 1997), 391.

PART IV: Writing Your Own Parable

Parable Principle 2

As described in chapter 1, parables contain two levels of meaning. There is the surface meaning of the actual story told and the deeper meaning to which the story points. So then, in Jesus' parables, what is the deeper level of meaning that each surface story points to? The deeper meaning is the revelation of the kingdom of God.

This principle is particularly important for understanding the parable of the dishonest manager because, on the surface, it seems to be encouraging dishonest behavior. In this parable, the surface meaning focuses on the manager's boldness. However, there is another meaning that goes far beyond the manager's actions. Again, Jesus' parables reveal the kingdom of God, and through this specific parable, he is telling us that since we are citizens of the kingdom of God, we should live accordingly.

We previously looked at three aspects about the kingdom of God. Choose one aspect that you would like to talk about in your parable. Think about how this aspect will structure your parable and write your reflections below.

____

____

____

____

____

____

____

____

____

____

____

3

The Father's Grace

In this chapter you will read a parable from Persia that describes the relationship between a father and his three sons. This parable teaches conventional wisdom through family relationships. You will also read a parable from Jesus that shows us the relationship between a father and his sons. However, Jesus' parable teaches something astonishing and different from conventional wisdom. Jesus uses the tender imagery of a father and his two sons to reveal the love of God's saving grace.

PART I: A Persian Parable

Before Reading Consider...

- What are some characteristics of a good father?
- What are some characteristics of a good son?
- How would you define the word "grace"?

The Father and His Three Sons

(1) Once there was a ruler of Persia who had three sons. He also had a beautiful pearl. Because a pearl cannot be divided, he wanted to choose one son to have it forever. He asked each son the same question, "What is the best deed you have done recently?"

(2) First the eldest son spoke. "Last week a man gave me some precious jewels to carry for him. He didn't even count the jewels, so I could easily have helped myself to some of them. But did I take any? No. I delivered them to the right person, as the merchant had asked me."

(3) "My son," said the father, "that's good but you couldn't have done anything else without feeling ashamed."

(4) Then the second son spoke. "As I walked past a lake the other day I saw a child playing. Suddenly he fell in as I watched. What did I do? I swam after him and saved his life."

(5) "My son," said the father again, "that's good but you couldn't have done anything else without feeling ashamed."

(6) Finally it was third son's turn to speak. "The other day, as I walked through the mountains, who should I see but a sleeping man. He had fallen asleep very close to the edge of a dangerous precipice.

(7) "I recognized him immediately. This man has hated me for a long time and done very unkind things to me. I wanted to keep walking but something inside me made me stop and go back to wake him. I knew he wouldn't understand why I woke him and I knew he would be angry with me. Sure enough when he woke he shouted at me angrily."

(8) "My son," said the father, "you did good without any hope of reward and you did it to someone who had done wrong to you. That is a really noble deed. This pearl is for you."

Notes/Questions

____

____

____

____

____

Grammar Focus[1]

Circle three organizational markers in the parable. Write them in the chart and then write the sentence each appears in.

Organizational Marker 1	Organizational Marker 2	Organizational Marker 3
Sentence:	Sentence:	Sentence:

1. For this section, you can check your work with the Answer Key found in the back of this book.

These organizational markers are all adverbs. Some adverbs are formed by adding the ending *–ly* to an adjective. For example, "Jorge is a fluent speaker in Spanish" can be changed to "Jorge speaks Spanish fluently".

Underline five *–ly* adverbs in the parable. Write the adverb below and write the sentence it appears in.

Example

Adverb: recently Sentence: What is the best deed you have done recently?

1) Adverb: __________ Sentence: ______________________________

____

2) Adverb: __________ Sentence: ______________________________

____

3) Adverb: __________ Sentence: ______________________________

____

4) Adverb: __________ Sentence: ______________________________

____

5) Adverb: __________ Sentence: ______________________________

____

Vocabulary Focus[2]

Match the word on the left with the definition on the right. In the blank provided, write the correct letter.

1) _____ beautiful	a) having high moral qualities or greatness
2) _____ precious	b) unsafe; likely to cause injury
3) _____ ashamed	c) of great value
4) _____ precipice	d) one who buys and sells things
5) _____ noble	e) pleasing to the eye; lovely
6) _____ jewels	f) steep cliff; overhanging rock
7) _____ merchant	g) to be sorry for something
8) _____ dangerous	h) valuable ring, necklace or gem

2. For this section, you can check your work with the Answer Key found in the back of this book.

Think-Pair-Share

Complete each of the following questions with one of the answers listed below. There could be more than one answer for each point. Compare answers with a partner.

1) The pearl was probably…

   quite valuable

   easy to replace

   quite cheap

2) The father wanted to give away the pearl…

   to encourage his sons to do the right thing

   because he didn't need the pearl

   out of curiosity about his sons' lives

3) At the end, the first and second sons might have felt…

   relieved

   jealous

   happy

4) At the end the third son probably felt…

   surprised

   embarrassed

   delighted

5) The father seemed to find the answer to his problem…

   quite easy

   very difficult

   time consuming

Theological Connection

1) In your opinion, did the father make the right decision? Why or why not?

   ____

   ____

   ____

   ____

2) Is this parable astonishing? Why or why not? If not, what is another adjective that can be used to describe the parable?

___

___

___

PART II: Furthering Your Knowledge

Keeping in mind the wisdom of this parable, read the following passage about God's grace. Read the left column if you want something more difficult or the right column for something easier.

As you read, underline parts you would like to ask questions about. Use the lines at the end of this reading to write down any questions you might have for your teacher.

Common Grace and Saving Grace

Difficult	Simplified
(1) "Grace is unmerited benevolence. A theological understanding of grace begins with the unearned favor that God extends to all humanity and to his chosen people."[3] That is, God gives his grace to all of us, even though none of us deserve it. However, as the quote suggests, there are differences in the grace that God gives to all people and the grace he gives specifically to the church. The first kind is often called common grace and the second kind saving grace. Any goodness in our fallen world comes from these undeserved graces. "Everything outside of hell is grace."[4]	(1) What is grace? It is favor that we don't deserve. Grace is free for every human being. We don't deserve it but God gives it to us.[3] There are two kinds of grace. We use the term common grace for the grace God gives to everyone. We use the term saving grace for what he gives to the church. All grace comes from God and the only place without grace is hell.[4]

3. Mark A. Bowald, "Grace" in Kevin J. Vanhoozer, ed., *Dictionary for Theological Interpretation of the Bible* (Grand Rapids, MI: Baker Academic, 2005), 268.

4. Gordon Fee, *People of the Presence*, Podcast audio, Redeemer Sermon Store, MP3, October 15, 2010, http://sermons.redeemer.com/store/index.cfm?fuseaction=display&Product_ID=18591.

(2) As discussed in chapter 1, sin has corrupted every part of creation, including every part of us. Paul declares, echoing Psalm 14, "...both Jews and Greeks, are under sin, as it is written: 'None is righteous, no, not one; no one understands; no one seeks for God... no one does good, not even one.'"[5] We might compare this to adding a drop of poison to a glass of water, which makes all of the liquid deadly. In the same way, sin has poisoned our nature, which was originally good. And like the poisoned water, our poisoned nature is also deadly because it makes us flee from God instead of seeking him.

(2) In chapter 1 we saw that every part of God's creation has been spoiled by sin. In Romans 3:9-12 Paul uses the words of Psalm 14 to tell us, "None is righteous, no, not one; no one understands; no one seeks for God... no one does good, not even one."[5] What happens if you add one drop of poison to a glass of water? All the water is poisoned. Our nature is like that. Once it was good but then it was poisoned. Now we run away from God instead of running to him.

(3) On the other hand, people's ideas and actions often agree with the commands of God. For instance, most people believe that it is good to help the poor and that it is wrong to steal. Common grace lets us reconcile these ideas and actions with our poisoned natures. This grace, which he gives to all people, both reduces the effects of sin and enables all people to affirm and create things that reflect God's truth, goodness, and beauty. Perhaps the most striking example of this is Paul's address at the Areopagus, when he describes God by saying, "In him we live and move and have our being."[6]

(3) But we also have ideas and we do things which follow God's rules. Most of us believe that it is good to help the poor and that it is wrong to steal.

By God's common grace all people can have these ideas and actions even though our natures are poisoned. Because of this grace the effects of our sin are lessened. Also all people are able to make and do things that reflect God's truth, goodness, and beauty. Listen to this great example in Paul's address at the Areopagus. He tells us about God in these words. "'In him we live and move and have our being."[6]

5. Romans 3:9-12.

6. Acts 17:28.

Surprisingly, Paul is quoting a pagan Greek writer in order to communicate truths about God. Only by God's grace could this ancient author have known this truth. Similarly, many other notable Christians have praised the wisdom that God's common grace has given to non-Christians. For example, Augustine commended Plato, Calvin commended Cicero, and C.S. Lewis commended Confucius.

(4) However, while common grace may give people the desire for wisdom, as it did for the Greeks who "seek wisdom," it cannot make us seek God. Instead, our poisoned natures will see "Christ…the wisdom of God" as "folly" or foolishness.[7] Christ challenges much conventional wisdom with surprising truths. For example, he tells us that, "Whoever finds his life will lose it, and whoever loses his life for my sake will find it."[8] Only saving grace, which he gives solely to his church, can make us seek the astonishing "wisdom of God," because, by this grace, this "unmerited benevolence," Christ first sought us.

It is surprising that Paul is quoting a non-Christian Greek writer to tell us truths about God. This ancient author could have known this truth only by God's grace. In the same way, many other famous Christians have praised the wisdom that God's common grace has given to non-Christians. For example, Augustine said good things about Plato, Calvin about Cicero, and C.S. Lewis about Confucius.

(4) However, while common grace may make people want wisdom, as it did for the Greeks who "seek wisdom," it cannot make us seek God. Instead, our poisoned natures will see "Christ…the wisdom of God" as "folly" or foolishness.[7] Christ challenges typical wisdom with surprising truths. For example, he tells us that, "Whoever finds his life will lose it, and whoever loses his life for my sake will find it."[8] Only saving grace can make us seek the amazing "wisdom of God," because, by this grace, Christ first sought us.

7. 1 Corinthians 1:22-25.

8. Matthew 10:39.

Notes/Questions

Think More About the Meaning

1) How does the Persian parable relate to common grace? Does it show wisdom?

2) How is the father's choice of the third son different from the grace of God?

3) Imagine that there is a fourth son who did a bad deed rather than a good one. What might his honest answer be to his father?

4) How could the father respond to the fourth son in a way that shows the "wisdom of God," as it is described in the article?

5) Would most people find your answer to Question 4 wise or foolish? Why?

____

____

____

____

A Covenant Common to all Creation

Below is a short reading on the biblical basis for common grace. Do not worry if you cannot understand every word or sentence. Try to read for the main idea. You may find it helpful to underline or highlight key words or phrases and to make notes in the margins. When you are finished, summarize the theological content of each paragraph in a single sentence.

Before you begin, write a short definition of the term covenant. If you have access to a theological dictionary, use that as a reference.

____

____

____

____

(1) Grace is not something that God infuses into us. As Michael Horton writes of grace, it "...is God's own attitude and action that he shows to those who deserve the very opposite."[9] The covenants that God has made with us are the channels through which we receive his grace. As John Frame remarks, "In a broad sense, all of God's dealings with creation are covenantal in character."[10] In particular, the covenant most directly connected to what we have called common grace is God's covenant with Noah. This is not the covenant between God and his elect, but a covenant between God and all of creation.

(2) After the flood receded, Noah offered burnt offerings to God. Then, after smelling the aroma of the burnt offering, God made a pledge to Noah, his sons, each of his future descendants, and every living thing on the earth. He said, "I establish my covenant with you, that never again shall all flesh be cut off by the waters of the flood, and never again shall there be a flood to destroy the earth."[11] This covenant demonstrates his grace towards us because such destruction is what we, in our sin, deserve. However, this is

9. Michael Horton, *Introducing Covenant Theology* (Grand Rapids, MI: Baker Academic, 2006), 156.

10. John M. Frame, *The Doctrine of the Knowledge of God* (Phillipsburg, NJ: Presbyterian and Reformed Publishing Company, 1987), 12.

11. Genesis 9:11

a covenant of common grace, not saving grace. "This is a unilateral oath that does not depend on what humans do, but it is not redemptive. It is a promise to uphold creation in its natural order, not to release it from sin and death."[12]

(3) Vern Poythress cites the effects of this covenant when Paul tells the people of Lystra that God has witnessed about himself by "...satisfying your hearts with food and gladness."[13] Though not all theologians may agree, Poythress roots common grace in the person and work of Christ. Commenting on Noah's offering, he writes, "These burnt offerings, like all the other sacrificial offerings by God's people in the Old Testament, prefigure the self-offering of Christ (Heb. 10:1–14)."[14] As Poythress explains, this covenant does not grant salvation, but through the work of Christ it "...gave a basis for lesser benefits, the benefits of common grace that come to unbelievers. As sinners against God, we all deserve to die immediately. But we still receive life and food and sunshine and other benefits..."

(4) There is also another way in which this covenant points us to Christ. After his promise God said, "I have set my bow in the cloud, and it shall be a sign of the covenant between me and the earth."[15] The sign is a rainbow but God describes it as a war bow. The *Jesus Storybook Bible* eloquently illustrates how this points to the suffering that Christ would endure for our sin:

> God's strong anger against hate and sadness and death would come down once more - but not on his people, or his world. No, God's war bow was not pointing down at his people. It was pointing up, into the heart of Heaven.[16]

Think-Pair Share

After reading this passage, how has your understanding of covenant changed? Share your response with a partner.

____

____

____

____

12. Horton, *Introducing Covenant Theology*, 106.
13. Vern Poythress, *In the Beginning was the Word: Language – A God-Centered Approach* (Wheaton, IL: Crossway, 2009), 119. The scripture quotation is from Acts 14:17.
14. Ibid.
15. Genesis 9:13.
16. Sally Lloyd-Jones, *The Jesus Storybook Bible: Every Story Whispers his Name* (Grand Rapids, MI: Zondervan, 2007), 47. Technically, this is a book for children, but it deserves to be read by the old as well as the young.

➲ Reading Strategy: Summarizing

Write a one-sentence summary of the theological content for each paragraph:

<u>*Example*</u>

1) The favor of God's common grace toward all of creation is established through covenant, which is demonstrated in God's covenant with Noah.

2) ______________________________

____

____

3) ______________________________

____

____

4) ______________________________

____

____

PART III: A Parable of Jesus

➲ Before Reading Consider…

What is the context, or the setting, in which a parable is told? Below is the context of one of Jesus' most famous parables:

> Now the tax collectors and sinners were all drawing near to hear him. And the Pharisees and the scribes grumbled, saying, "This man receives sinners and eats with them."
>
> So he told them this parable... (Luke 15:1-3)

Jesus tells his parable to two very different groups of people. Use the chart on the following page to make some notes about the context and the two groups in Jesus' audience.

Questions	Group 1	Group 2
Who are they?	The tax collectors and sinners	The Pharisees and the scribes
How does this group seem to feel about the other group?		
What does each group think about Jesus?		
Does the attitude of this group make Jesus tell the parable? Why or why not?		
Does Jesus want to change the attitude of this group with the parable? Why or why not?		

In his book *The Prodigal God*, Timothy Keller writes:

> So to whom is Jesus' teaching in this parable directed? It is to the second group, the scribes and Pharisees. It is in response to their attitude that Jesus begins to tell the parable. The parable of the two sons takes an extended look at the soul of the elder brother and climaxes with a powerful plea for him to change his heart.[17]

17. Timothy Keller, *The Prodigal God* (New York, NY: Dutton, 2008), 9.

The parable we will study is commonly called the parable of the prodigal son, which suggests that only the younger son is lost. However, based on the parable's context, what might be a better name for this parable?

____

____

The Parable of the Prodigal Son

And he said, "There was a man who had two sons. And the younger of them said to his father, 'Father, give me the share of property that is coming to me.' And he divided his property between them. Not many days later, the younger son gathered all he had and took a journey into a far country, and there he squandered his property in reckless living. And when he had spent everything, a severe famine arose in that country, and he began to be in need. So he went and hired himself out to one of the citizens of that country, who sent him into his fields to feed pigs. And he was longing to be fed with the pods that the pigs ate, and no one gave him anything.

"But when he came to himself, he said, 'How many of my father's hired servants have more than enough bread, but I perish here with hunger! I will arise and go to my father, and I will say to him, "Father, I have sinned against heaven and before you. I am no longer worthy to be called your son. Treat me as one of your hired servants."' And he arose and came to his father. But while he was still a long way off, his father saw him and felt compassion, and ran and embraced him and kissed him. And the son said to him, 'Father, I have sinned against heaven and before you. I am no longer worthy to be called your son.' But the father said to his servants, 'Bring quickly the best robe, and put it on him, and put a ring on his hand, and shoes on his feet. And bring the fattened calf and kill it, and let us eat and celebrate. For this my son was dead, and is alive again; he was lost, and is found.' And they began to celebrate.

"Now his older son was in the field, and as he came and drew near to the house, he heard music and dancing. And he called one of the servants and asked what these things meant. And he said to him, 'Your brother has come, and your father has killed the fattened calf, because he has received him back safe and sound.' But he was angry and refused to go in. His father came out and entreated him, but he answered his father, 'Look, these many years I have served you, and I never disobeyed your command, yet you never gave me a young goat, that I might celebrate with my friends. But when this son of yours came, who has devoured your property with prostitutes, you killed the fattened calf for him!' And he said to him, 'Son, you are always with me, and all that is mine is yours. It was fitting to celebrate and be glad, for this your brother was dead, and is alive; he was lost, and is found.'"

(Luke 15:11-32)

Vocabulary Focus[18]

Underline the following words in Jesus' parable. Write a definition for the word in the line provided. Before referring to your dictionary, use the context of the word to help you define it. Then write a sentence. Some of these words appear more than once in the parable.

Example

divided

Definition: Separate into parts

Sentence: He divided his land into two sections.

1) squandered

   Definition: ____________________

   Sentence: ____________________

2) reckless

   Definition: ____________________

   Sentence: ____________________

3) hired

   Definition: ____________________

   Sentence: ____________________

4) embraced

   Definition: ____________________

   Sentence: ____________________

5) celebrate

   Definition: ____________________

   Sentence: ____________________

6) disobeyed

   Definition: ____________________

   Sentence: ____________________

7) devoured

   Definition: ____________________

   Sentence: ____________________

18. For this section, you can check your work with the Answer Key found in the back of this book.

➲ Key Issues

When the younger son said, "Father, give me the share of the property that is coming to me." He was demanding his inheritance. However, a child only receives an inheritance when his or her parents die. Therefore, the son was communicating that he loved the father's resources more than the father's life.

1) How would you expect the father to respond to the son's request?

____

____

____

____

2) Eventually the younger son decided to return home and to tell his father, "I am no longer worthy to be called your son. Treat me as one of your hired servants." He wanted to work as a hired servant to pay his debt to his father. Do you think the son deserved to be treated like a son or a like a hired servant? Why?

____

____

____

____

3) Did the father let him pay back the debt by becoming a hired servant? What happened instead?

____

____

____

After the younger son came home, the older son responded disrespectfully when the father invited him to the feast. The older son was angry and told his father, "Look, these many years I have served you, and I never disobeyed your command, yet you never gave me a young goat, that I might celebrate with my friends."

4) Based on his response, did the older son care more about the father's resources or the father's life? Why?

____

____

____

____

5) The older brother wanted the things that he thought he deserved from the father. He related to the father like a hired-servant. How was his attitude toward his father similar to the plan of the younger son?

____

6) The two sons related to the father in the same way.[19] They both wanted to be workers instead of sons. The younger son wanted to pay off his debt to the father and the older son wanted to put the father in his debt. Why did they want to do this?

____

7) At the end of the parable, which son was still *lost*? How does this relate to the earlier discussion of the parable's context in Luke 15:1-3?

____

8) How does the father's response to his younger son demonstrate the "wisdom of God" and relate to saving grace?

____

19. Keller, *The Prodigal God*, 35-36.

PART IV: Writing Your Own Parable

Parable Principle 3
The characters of parables are usually human. Some of Jesus' parables focus on things like birds, seeds, and weeds. However, in contrast to a fable, these things are not given human characteristics.

Use the chart below to make some notes about the characters in Jesus' parable.

	Who does he represent?	What are his characteristics?	Necessary for the parable because...
The Father			
The Younger Son			
The Older Son			

1) Why do these parables focus on the relationships between fathers and their sons?

____

____

____

____

2) Jesus' parables reveal the kingdom of God to his audiences and the father in the parable of the two sons represents God. Complete the two sentences contrasting the kingdom of God with the kingdom in the Persian parable, which is similar to all kingdoms of man.

   a) In the kingdom of man ______________________________
   but in the kingdom of God ______________________________.

   b) In the kingdom of man ______________________________
   but in the kingdom of God ______________________________.

Based on the beliefs, attitudes, or behaviors you would like to change with your parable, decide who your characters will be. Use the following chart to create several characters for your parable.

	Who does he or she represent?	What are his or her characteristics?	Necessary for the parable because...
Character #1			
Character #2			
Character #3			
Character #4			

4

The Perfect Prophet

In this chapter you will read a parable from Nathan, an Old Testament prophet. You will examine how parables use indirect communication to achieve their purposes in their audiences. After learning about Christ's fulfillment of the Old Testament, you will then see how Christ, who is the perfect prophet, tells parables similar to the prophet Nathan. That is, Christ tells intriguing stories that make his audience see issues from new perspectives.

PART I: A Parable from 2 Samuel

Before Reading Consider...

- What is your most treasured possession?
- How would you feel if someone stole it?
- What would you say to the person who stole it?

David and Nathan

(1) And the LORD sent Nathan to David. He came to him and said to him, "There were two men in a certain city, the one rich and the other poor. The rich man had very many flocks and herds but the poor man had nothing but one little ewe lamb, which he had bought. And he brought it up, and it grew up with him and with his children. It used to eat of his morsel and drink from his cup and lie in his arms, and it was like a daughter to him. Now there came a traveler to the rich man, and he was unwilling to take one of his own flock or herd to prepare for the guest who had come to him, but he took the poor man's lamb and prepared it for the man who had come to him."

(2) Then David's anger was greatly kindled against the man, and he said to Nathan, "As the LORD lives, the man who has done this deserves to die, and he shall restore the lamb fourfold, because he did this thing, and because he had no pity."

(3) Nathan said to David, "You are the man! Thus says the LORD, the God of Israel, 'I anointed you king over Israel, and I delivered you out of the hand of Saul. And I gave you your master's house and your master's wives into your arms and gave you the house of Israel and of Judah. And if this were too little, I would add to you as much more. Why have you despised the word of the LORD, to do what is evil in his sight? You have struck down Uriah the Hittite with the sword and have taken his wife to be your wife and have killed him with the sword of the Ammonites. Now therefore the sword shall never depart from your house, because you have despised me and have taken the wife of Uriah the Hittite to be your wife.' Thus says the LORD, 'Behold, I will raise up evil against you out of your own house. And I will take your wives before your eyes and give them to your neighbor, and he shall lie with your wives in the sight of this sun. For you did it secretly, but I will do this thing before all Israel and before the sun.'"

(4) David said to Nathan, "I have sinned against the LORD."

(5) And Nathan said to David, "The LORD also has put away your sin; you shall not die. Nevertheless, because by this deed you have utterly scorned the LORD, the child who is born to you shall die." Then Nathan went to his house.

(2 Samuel 12:1-15)

Notes/Questions

____

Theological Connection

1) Why do you think Nathan told David a parable instead of accusing him directly?

2) Nathan is a prophet and one of the roles of a prophet is to speak out against injustice. Find another example in which a prophet from the Old Testament does this and explain how it is similar to Nathan's confrontation with David.

____

____

____

____

3) In the Old Testament, a major role of a prophet was to tell people about the coming of the Messiah. Earlier, in 2 Samuel 7, Nathan is sent by God to tell David that the Messiah will be one of David's descendants. Read this chapter and then explain some differences between Nathan and David's interaction in 2 Samuel 7 and 2 Samuel 12.

____

____

____

____

➲ Reading Strategy[1]

Read the following description of parables by N.T. Wright. Like the story told by the prophet Nathan, this passage is written in strong, eloquent language. Fill in the boxes on the following page with notes about the passage.

> Where head-on attack would certainly fail, the parable hides the wisdom of the serpent behind the innocence of the dove, gaining entrance and favor which can then be used to change assumptions which the hearer would otherwise keep hidden away for safety. Nathan tells David a story about a rich man, a poor man, and a little lamb; David is enraged; and Nathan springs the trap.[2]

---

1. For this section, you can check your work with the Answer Key found in the back of this book.

2. N.T. Wright, *The New Testament and the People of God. Vol. 1 of Christian Origins and the Question of God.* (Minneapolis, MN: Fortress Press, 1992), 40.

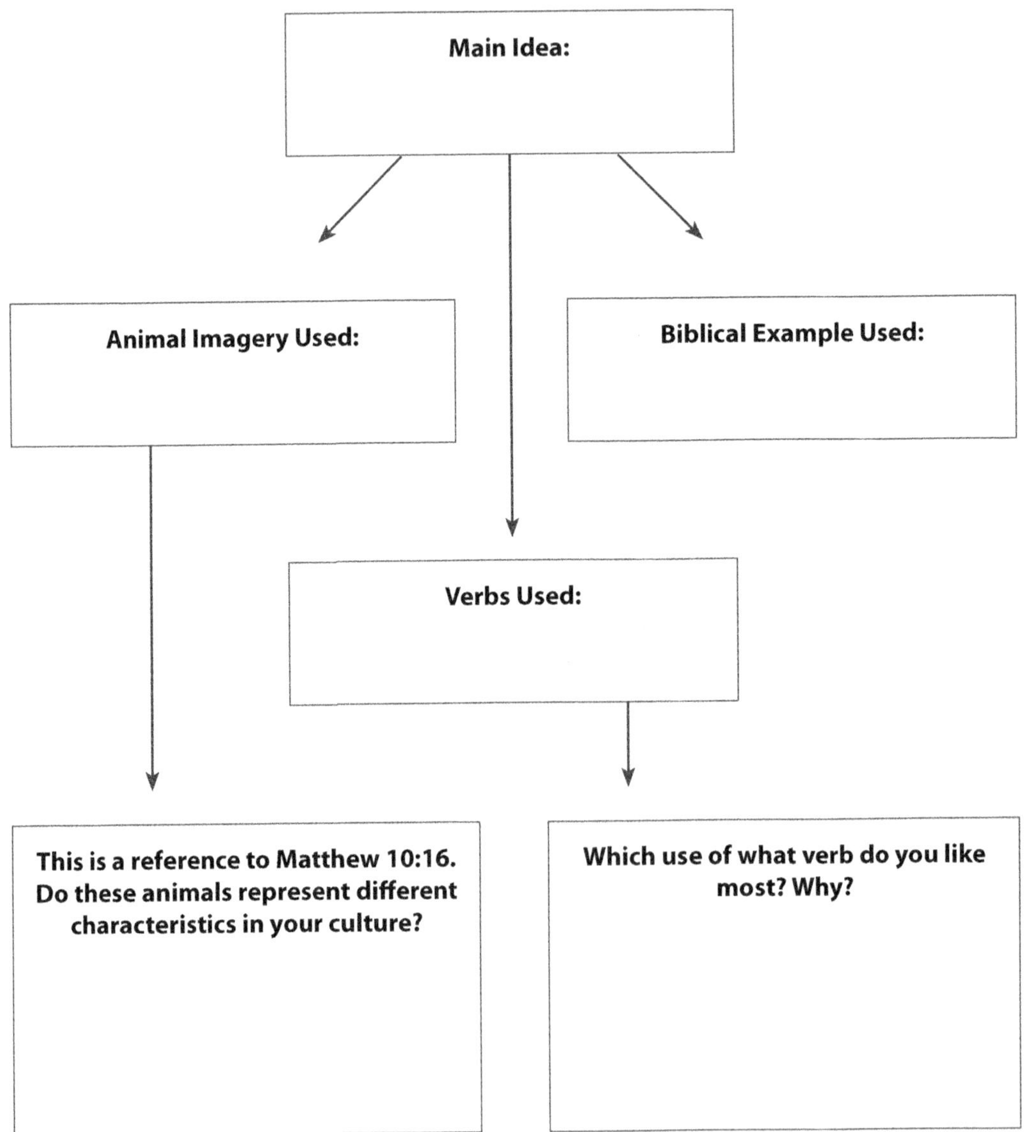

PART II: Furthering Your Knowledge

Keeping in mind the roles of a prophet, read the following passage about Christ, the perfect prophet. Read the left column if you want something more difficult or the right column for something easier.

As you read, underline parts you would like to ask questions about. Use the lines at the end of this reading to write down any questions you might have for your teacher.

Christ, Typology, and the Prophets

Difficult	Simplified
(1) As Jesus walked with the two travelers on their way to Emmaus, he talked with them: "And beginning with Moses and all the Prophets, he interpreted to them in all the Scriptures the things concerning himself."[3] The travelers needed to see Jesus as the fulfillment of the Old Testament to correctly understand his person and work. Of course, we must do the same. However, like the pair going to Emmaus, we often forget that Christ warned, "Do not think that I have come to abolish the Law or the Prophets; I have not come to abolish them but to fulfill them."[4] The hermeneutical, or interpretative, practice of typology helps us heed this warning.	(1) As Jesus and two travelers walked on the Emmaus road he talked to them. He told them the meaning of the passages in the Old Testament that talk about him.[3] Why did he talk like that? Because if the travelers were going to understand Jesus, they needed to know what people had written about him already. We must also understand how Christ fulfills the Old Testament. However, sometimes we make the same mistake as the travelers. We must remember Jesus' warning when he said, "Do not think that I have come to abolish the Law or the Prophets; I have not come to abolish them but to fulfill them."[4]
(2) Typology interprets Christ as the perfection of different roles that are present in the Old Testament. Theologian Kevin Vanhoozer explains this practice well, writing, "The New Testament as a whole employs a diversity of types that, taken together, virtually recapitulates the whole of the Old Testament: Jesus is the second Adam, a prophet greater than Moses, a priest of the order of Melchizedek, a Davidic king."[5]	(2) The Old Testament writers refer to Christ many times. Then in the New Testament we learn the complete story of Jesus' person and work. This complete story helps us understand how Christ fulfills the Old Testament. For instance, the interpretative practice of typology helps us understand how Christ relates to those who came before him in the Old Testament. It's like this: OT — NT Adam — Jesus is the 2nd Adam Moses — Jesus is a greater prophet Melchizedek — Jesus is also a priest David — Jesus is a king like David[5]

3. Luke 24:27.

4. Matthew 5:15.

5. Kevin Vanhoozer, *The Drama of Doctrine: A Canonical-Linguistic Approach to Christian Theology* (Louisville, KY: Westminster John Knox Press, 2005), 222.

The final three "types" that Vanhoozer mentions, those of prophet, priest, and king, are often called the threefold office of Christ. John Calvin, in particular, demonstrated the importance of these three offices to understanding Christ's person and work. To illustrate this hermeneutical importance, let us examine the office of prophet.

That means Christ is a prophet, priest and king. John Calvin told us how important these three roles are.

(3) One of the passages that Calvin cites concerning Jesus' prophetic ministry is the beginning of Hebrews. These verses read, "Long ago, at many times and in many ways, God spoke to our fathers by the prophets, but in these last days he has spoken to us by his Son..."[6] Therefore, in comparing Jesus to all other prophets, Calvin writes that God "...exalted him by a singular privilege beyond the rank of all others."[7] Jesus fulfilled the office of prophet by giving us the full revelation of the gospel, which was only partially supplied by previous prophets.

(3) Where do we read about Jesus the prophet? Take for example the beginning of Hebrews. It says, "Long ago, at many times and in many ways, God spoke to our fathers by the prophets, but in these last days he has spoken to us by his Son..."[6] Calvin tells us that Jesus, the Son of God, is the greatest of all prophets.[7] Jesus the prophet gave us all of the good news (the gospel). Before that we had only part of the good news.

(4) In particular, the gospel according to Luke seems to illustrate this movement from earlier prophets to Jesus in its first two chapters. As Michael Wilcock states, "...both these opening chapters of the gospel are taken up with the thought that after four centuries in which the voice of prophecy has been silent, now at last God speaks again, through 'the tongues of men and of angels.'"[8]

(4) In the gospel of Luke the first two chapters move from earlier prophets to Jesus. Michael Wilcock says that chapters 1 and 2 show something new. After 400 years without the voices of prophets, now at last God speaks again, through men and angels.[8]

---

6. Hebrews 1:1-2.

7. John Calvin, *Institutes of the Christian Religion*, ed. John T. McNeill, trans. Ford Lewis Battles (Louisville, KY: Westminster John Knox Press, 1960), 2.15.2.

8. Michael Wilcock, *The Savior of the World: the Message of Luke's Gospel. The Bible Speaks Today* Series, ed. John Stott. (Downers Grove, IL: InterVarsity Press, 1979) 45-46. The closing quotation is from 1 Corinthians 13:1 and Wilcock is quoting the Revised Standard Version of the Bible.

(5) Angels, Mary, Elizabeth, Zachariah, Simeon, and Anna, each in turn, prophesy about the child who is the Son of God. Then, at the end of the second chapter, the child himself speaks. After days of searching, his parents find him in the temple and he gives them a reply they do not understand, saying, "Why were you looking for me? Did you not know that I must be in my Father's house?"[9] Even as a child, Jesus declares that he is the Son of God, an identity that makes him the greatest of all prophets. This is why, in Luke's first specific example of his public ministry, Jesus can boldly proclaim that the words of another prophet, Isaiah, have been fulfilled on that very day.[10]

(5) Angels, Mary, Elizabeth, Zachariah, Simeon, and Anna, each in turn, prophesy about the child who is the Son of God. Then, at the end of the second chapter, the child himself speaks. After days of searching, his parents find him in the temple. What does he say to them?

"Why were you looking for me? Did you not know that I must be in my Father's house?"[9] Even as a child, Jesus says those words. Because he is the Son of God, he is the greatest of all prophets. This is why, when Luke speaks for the first time about Jesus' public ministry, Jesus can boldly say that the words of another prophet, Isaiah, have come true on that day.[10]

Notes/Questions

9. Luke 2:49.
10. Luke 4:16-21.

Word Selection[11]

Without looking back at the reading, fill in each blank with the correct word from the word bank. Use each word only once.

Word Bank

identity, typology, threefold, priest, fulfillment, interpretive, prophet

1) The travelers needed to see Jesus as the ______________________ of the Old Testament to correctly understand his person and work.

2) The hermeneutical, or ________________________ practice of typology helps us heed this warning.

3) ______________________ interprets Christ as the perfection of different roles that are present in the Old Testament.

4) The final three "types" that Vanhoozer mentions, those of prophet, ________________, and king, are often called the ________________ office of Christ.

5) Jesus fulfilled the office of ____________________ by giving us the full revelation of the gospel.

6) Even as a child, Jesus declares that he is the Son of God, an ________________ that makes him the greatest of all prophets.

Think-Pair-Share: Creating a Role Play

Imagine being one of the two people listening to Jesus as you walk down the road to Emmaus. First, read the passage on the next page. Then, one partner asks the question to Jesus and the other partner answers it. Based on the example, complete the conversation with your partner and then present it to the class.

11. For this section, you can check your work with the Answer Key found in the back of this book.

That very day two of them were going to a village named Emmaus, about seven miles from Jerusalem, and they were talking with each other about all these things that had happened. While they were talking and discussing together, Jesus himself drew near and went with them. But their eyes were kept from recognizing him. And he said to them, "What is this conversation that you are holding with each other as you walk?" And they stood still, looking sad. Then one of them, named Cleopas, answered him, "Are you the only visitor to Jerusalem who does not know the things that have happened there in these days?" And he said to them, "What things?" And they said to him, "Concerning Jesus of Nazareth, a man who was a prophet mighty in deed and word before God and all the people, and how our chief priests and rulers delivered him up to be condemned to death, and crucified him. But we had hoped that he was the one to redeem Israel. Yes, and besides all this, it is now the third day since these things happened. Moreover, some women of our company amazed us. They were at the tomb early in the morning, and when they did not find his body, they came back saying that they had even seen a vision of angels, who said that he was alive. Some of those who were with us went to the tomb and found it just as the women had said, but him they did not see." And he said to them, "O foolish ones, and slow of heart to believe all that the prophets have spoken! Was it not necessary that the Christ should suffer these things and enter into his glory?" And beginning with Moses and all the Prophets, he interpreted to them in all the Scriptures the things concerning himself.

So they drew near to the village to which they were going. He acted as if he were going farther, but they urged him strongly, saying, "Stay with us, for it is toward evening and the day is now far spent." So he went in to stay with them. When he was at table with them, he took the bread and blessed and broke it and gave it to them. And their eyes were opened, and they recognized him. And he vanished from their sight. They said to each other, "Did not our hearts burn within us while he talked to us on the road, while he opened to us the Scriptures?" And they rose that same hour and returned to Jerusalem. And they found the eleven and those who were with them gathered together, saying, "The Lord has risen indeed, and has appeared to Simon!" Then they told what had happened on the road, and how he was known to them in the breaking of the bread.

(Luke 24:13-37)

Create the Role Play

A: What are you talking about?

B: We are talking about Jesus of Nazareth. Haven't you heard what has happened?

A: What are you saying about him?

B:

A:

B:

A:

B:

A:

B:

A:

B:

Think More About the Meaning

1) How does typology connect the New Testament to the Old Testament?

____

____

____

____

2) Find a passage in the Gospels in which Jesus, the perfect prophet, spoke out boldly against injustice with a parable, as Nathan did to David. Summarize what happened in the passage.

____

____

____

____

3) At the end of Nathan's parable and explanation, David says, "I have sinned against the LORD." Find a passage in which Jesus brings someone to repentance. Summarize what happened.

____

____

____

____

PART III: A Parable of Jesus

Before Reading Consider...

As you read the following parable of Jesus, remember that prophets are powerful communicators. They speak effectively to their audience. Read the following chart and answer the questions in the bottom row.

Nathan	Jesus
Who was his audience? When David was young, he was a shepherd.	**Who was his audience?** Jesus lived in an agricultural society, in which everyone was familiar with farming.
Why would he tell a parable about sheep?	**Why would he tell a parable about seeds?**

The Parable of the Sower

And when a great crowd was gathering and people from town after town came to him, he said in a parable, "A sower went out to sow his seed. And as he sowed, some fell along the path and was trampled underfoot, and the birds of the air devoured it. And some fell on the rock, and as it grew up, it withered away, because it had no moisture. And some fell among thorns, and the thorns grew up with it and choked it. And some fell into good soil and grew and yielded a hundredfold." As he said these things, he called out, "He who has ears to hear, let him hear."

And when his disciples asked him what this parable meant, he said, "To you it has been given to know the secrets of the kingdom of God, but for others they are in parables, so that 'seeing they may not see, and hearing they may not understand.' Now the parable is this: The seed is the word of God. The ones along the path are those who have heard; then the devil comes and takes away the word from their hearts, so that they may not believe and be saved. And the ones on the rock are those who, when they hear the word, receive it with joy. But these have no root; they believe for a while, and in time of testing fall away. And as for what fell among the thorns, they are those who hear, but as they go on their way they are choked by the cares and riches and pleasures of life, and their fruit does not mature. As for that in the good soil, they are those who, hearing the word, hold it fast in an honest and good heart, and bear fruit with patience."

(Luke 8:1-15)

Personal Reflection

1) This is often called the parable of the sower, but many commentators have suggested that it be called something like the parable of the four soils. Why do you think they feel this way?

___

___

___

2) At the end of the parable Jesus says, "He who has ears to hear, let him hear." Judging by what Jesus does and says next, describe those who have "ears to hear."

___

___

___

3) As stated above, prophets are effective communicators. However, throughout the Bible, people often ignore, misunderstand, or attack their prophetic words. How does Jesus' parable illustrate these responses?

____

____

____

4) In response to Nathan's parable, David commands the guilty man to "restore the lamb fourfold." However, in Jesus' parable the good soil "yielded a hundredfold." Unlike the increase that David describes, the one that Jesus describes is beyond our ability. Who is responsible for this hundredfold increase? How does it happen?

____

____

____

5) Read the account of Simon the Magician in Acts 8:9-25. What kind of soil does Simon appear to be?

____

____

____

Grammar Focus: Indirect Speech[12]

If you report what another person has stated, you usually do not use the speaker's exact words (direct speech). Rather, you use reported or indirect speech. It is important to know how to transform direct speech into indirect speech. The structure may be different depending on whether you want to transform a statement, question or request. When transforming statements you may need to change pronouns, present tense verbs, place and time expressions or tenses. Two examples follow:

In Acts 8:19 Simon says, "Give me this power also, so that anyone on whom I lay my hands may receive the Holy Spirit." Follow the five steps listed below to turn this quotation into indirect speech.

1) Imperatives are introduced by <u>to</u> or <u>not to</u>
   - "give" becomes <u>to give</u>
2) Pronouns take third person forms
   - "me" becomes <u>him</u>; "I" becomes <u>he</u>; "my" becomes <u>his</u>

12. For this section, you can check your work with the Answer Key found in the back of this book.

3) "This" changes to <u>that</u> and "these" changes to <u>those</u>
4) Replace "may" with a past tense modal
   - "may receive" becomes <u>might receive</u>
5) Put lay in the past tense
   - "lay" becomes <u>laid</u>

Use these answers to fill in the blanks to change the above quotation into indirect speech.

Simon said __________ __________ __________ power also, so that anyone on
1 2 3

whom __________ __________ __________ hands __________ the Holy Spirit.
2 5 2 4

a) Peter, in his response to Simon's request, says in verse 21, "You have neither part nor lot in this matter, for your heart is not right before God." Follow the four steps listed below to turn this quotation into indirect speech.
   1) This example of indirect speech is introduced by <u>that</u>
   2) Pronouns take third person forms
      - "you" becomes <u>he</u>
      - "your" becomes <u>his</u>
   3) "This" and "these" change to <u>that</u> and <u>those</u> respectively
      - "this" becomes <u>that</u>
   4) Have and is change to past tense
      - "have" becomes <u>had</u>
      - "is" becomes <u>was</u>

Use these answers to fill in the blanks to change the above quotation into indirect speech.

Peter told Simon __________ __________ __________ neither part nor lot in
1 2 4

__________ matter, for __________ heart __________ not right before God.
3 2 4

b) Write a short paragraph using the answers from the grammar focus. Relate this passage of Acts to Jesus' parable, explaining what kind of soil best describes Simon the Magician. In your paragraph use your examples of indirect speech as evidence.

Key Issues: Prophets of the Past

While explaining the parable to his disciples, Jesus refers to the words of another prophet. In Isaiah 6:9 God instructs Isaiah to tell the people of Israel, "Keep on hearing, but do not understand; keep on seeing, but do not perceive." This connects Jesus' mission with Isaiah's prophetic ministry. Even more, Paul quotes these same words in his final address recorded in Acts.[13] From this we see that the church carries on the prophetic ministry that has been fulfilled in Christ.

Find two more examples from the New Testament in which members of the church tell people that the promised Messiah, who fulfills the Old Testament, has arrived. Such proclamation is one way to perform the role of a prophet. Complete the chart on the following page with two more examples.

13. Acts 28:25-27.

Passage	What happened?
Acts 28:17-28	Paul explained the person and work of Christ by interpreting the law of Moses and the prophets to the Jewish leaders in Rome. He told them that Jesus had fulfilled these scriptures.

Making Connections: Prophets of the Present

We as the church are "...also called to participate in the prophetic act through witnessing of the person and work of Jesus Christ."[14] To do this we must recognize that Jesus is not only the true fulfillment of the Old Testament but also the true fulfillment of every worldview. N.T. Wright identifies Jesus as the subversive fulfillment of the first-century-Jewish worldview.[15] That is, Jesus fulfilled his audience's hopes and expectations, but in a way they never would have expected, which forced them to reinterpret their entire history. However, in a general sense, all cultures find themselves in a similar situation. As Kevin Vanhoozer writes, "Jesus Christ is the hermeneutical key not only to the history of Israel but to the history of the whole world, and hence to the meaning of life, for he is the Logos through whom all things were created."[16] With that said, think about how Jesus the Messiah subversively fulfills your culture's worldview.

We might outline this subversive fulfillment as a two-step process. Jesus first *contradicts* the culture and secondly he *completes* it.[17] In the steps below, this process has

14. David W. Pao, "Prophecy and Prophets in the NT" in Kevin J. Vanhoozer, ed., *Dictionary for Theological Interpretation of the Bible* (Grand Rapids, MI: Baker Academic, 2005), 625.

15. Wright, *The New Testament and the People of God*, 40-41, 50, 67, 375, 379, 395-405, 471.

16. Vanhoozer, *The Drama of Doctrine*, 223.

17. This process and the two examples (ancient Greek and mainstream American culture) are taken from Timothy Keller, *Writing from a Christian Worldview*, Podcast audio. Redeemer Sermon Store, MP3, March 31, 2013, http://sermons2.redeemer.com/sermons/writing-christian-worldviewhttp://sermons.redeemer.com/store/index.cfm?fuseaction=display&Product_ID=18591 . Also see his *Center Church: Doing Balanced, Gospel-centered Ministry in your City* (Grand Rapids, MI: Zondervan, 2012), 111-112.

been outlined using the first-century-Greek culture as an example, according to Paul's description in 1 Corinthians 1:22-25.

Step 1: Jesus contradicts culture.

a) Greeks desire wisdom.

b) They see "Christ crucified" as foolishness, the very opposite of wisdom.

Step 2: Jesus completes the culture.

a) The eyes of the Greeks are opened. They realize their foolishness and recognize Christ as true wisdom, "the wisdom of God."

b) They reinterpret their life according to Christ, who has subversively fulfilled their worldview.

Complete the following chart of this two-step process using your own culture. An example, using mainstream American culture, has been provided in the middle column. Write your answers in the third column.

Question	Example	Your Answer
What is your culture?	Mainstream American culture	
What is a desire or expectation of your culture?	My culture desires freedom.	
How does Jesus contradict your culture?	My culture sees "Christ crucified" as slavery, the opposite of freedom. My culture thinks Jesus burdens people with rules to stop them from doing what they want to do.	

How does Jesus subversively fulfill a desire or expectation of your culture?	Only Jesus gives us true freedom, which is freedom from sin.	
How does Jesus reinterpret your history?	I always believed I was free, but I was actually a slave of sin.	

Look back over the answers to the questions above. How might your answers help you to talk about Christ in your culture?

____

____

____

PART IV: Writing Your Own Parable

Parable Principle 4
Parables are a form of indirect communication. Instead of directly confronting a belief, attitude, or behavior present in their audience, parables use much more subtle means. They are stories that attract and hold the interest of their hearers. These hearers are so absorbed in the story that they do not realize they have been confronted until the story is over. Having listened attentively, the audience, to their surprise, has seen an issue from a new perspective.

➲ Compelling Stories

Commenting specifically on Nathan's parable, John Frame encourages us to be more attentive to when this kind of indirect communication is most useful for theological instruction. Pointing out that this method requires "artistry and nuance," he writes, "Nathan did not simply repeat the law; he told a story. That story had the effect of shaking David out of his rationalization, of helping him to make different patterns out of the facts, to call things by their right names."[18]

18. Frame, *The Doctrine of the Knowledge of God*, 157-8.

1) Why is it important for parables to be "compellingly interesting"[19] to "shake people out of their rationalizations?"

____

____

____

Parables are very short stories and so their structure is relatively simple. Most show how a character or characters resolve some crisis that has disturbed some prior peacefulness. However, sometimes their tellers intentionally withhold their endings. When this happens, the audience is given the opportunity to resolve a parable's plot with their own actions. For instance, in the parable of the prodigal son, we are not told if the older son accepts the father's invitation to the party. The parable serves as a kind of invitation to the Pharisees, who are represented by the older brother, to rejoice with the tax collectors and sinners, who are represented by the younger brother.

2) How does David "resolve the plot" of Nathan's parable? How does this help to accomplish Nathan's purpose in telling the parable?

____

____

____

Reading Strategy: Stages of a Parable

Generally speaking, stories have three basic stages:

1) The characters exist in some degree of peace with which they are content.
2) This peace is disrupted by a crisis that demands responsive action from a character or characters.
3) The responsive action resolves the crisis, often bringing about better circumstances than the initial peace of stage 1.

Even the story of the entire universe follows this framework, which has often been understood as a three-stage process of (1) creation, (2) fall, and (3) redemption. Regarding Jesus' parables, some have all three stages and some do not.[20] For instance, the parable of the good Samaritan does, whereas the parable of the prodigal son does not, because it

19. Snodgrass, *Stories with Intent*, 8.

20. The parable of the sower, one of the few parables that does not focus on human characters, veers from these three stages. It is possible that an interpreter could apply the stages to the growth of the seeds in each soil. However, the general parable principle we are focusing on is indirect communication through narrative, which still applies to this parable.

does not fully progress through stage 3. At the end, the crisis is only partially resolved. One son has been reconciled to the father, but the other has not. As described above, this parable invites the audience to complete stage 3 with their own actions.

We could apply these stages to the parable of the good Samaritan as follows:

1) A man is walking from Jerusalem to Jericho.
2) He is attacked by robbers and left injured on the side of the road.
3) After two others refuse to act with compassion, a Samaritan shows mercy to the man and uses his resources to heal the man's injuries.

➡ Describing the Stages

Now choose another one of Jesus' parables and likewise apply these three stages to it:

1) ______________________________

____

____

____

____

2) ______________________________

____

____

____

____

____

3) ______________________________

____

____

____

____

Now think about the parable you are writing. Structure your story using these three basic story stages. Depending on your purpose, you may leave stage 3 resolved or unresolved. And remember, parables are most successful when they are "compellingly interesting," so try to create a story that would interest your intended audience.

1) ______________________________

____

____

____

____

2) ______________________________

____

____

____

____

3) ______________________________

____

____

____

____

5

Persons, Purposes, and Persistence

In this chapter you will read a traditional Chinese parable. Then you will learn about Christ's plan for all of creation, a purpose that must be the final standard by which we interpret every event of our life. Finally, using a helpful interpretative process, you will examine a parable of Jesus in which he shows that the surety of this purpose should give us faith in every hardship.

PART I: A Chinese Parable

Before Reading Consider...

- What is some good news you recently received and how did you respond to it?
- What is some bad news you recently received and how did you respond to it?
- Do you think your responses were wise? Why or why not?

The Farmer

(1) A Chinese farmer gets a horse, which soon runs away. A neighbor says, "That's bad news." The farmer replies, "Good news, bad news, who can say?" The horse comes back and brings another horse with him. Good news, you might say.

(2) The farmer gives the second horse to his son, who rides it, then is thrown and badly breaks his leg. "So sorry for your bad news," says the concerned neighbor. "Good news, bad news, who can say?" the farmer replies.

(3) In a week or so, the emperor's men come and take every able-bodied young man to fight in a war. The farmer's son is spared. Good news, of course.

Notes/Questions

Theological Connection

1) What teaching does this parable offer its readers?

2) How would you have responded to each of the three situations in the story?

3) Is there wisdom in the farmer's responses? How wise (or unwise) are the farmer's answers?

Learning from the Parable

The farmer's responses remind us that judging too fast can be foolish. Often we give meaning to events too quickly and do not understand them in light of their larger context. Looking at any one event by itself, isolated from all others, stops us from seeing the whole story to which the event belongs. For example, when we read a novel, we understand it best by reading all of it. This gives us the whole story and the story is what gives order and unity to each of the novel's individual events. Stories supply their events with meaning. Consider the following example and its hasty interpreters.

Reflecting on the death of Jesus, the travelers on the Emmaus road said, "But we had hoped that he was the one to redeem Israel."[1] The event of Jesus' death on the cross had destroyed their hopes of redemption. They saw it as a tragedy. However, it was part of a redemption plan not just for Israel, but for all of creation. The resurrected Jesus rebuked their hasty judgment by showing them that his death must be understood as part of the Bible's whole story. Think about his answer:

> And he said to them, "O foolish ones, and slow of heart to believe all that the prophets have spoken! Was it not necessary that the Christ should suffer these things and enter into his glory?" And beginning with Moses and all the Prophets, he interpreted to them in all the Scriptures the things concerning himself.[2]

And so Jesus' death on the cross, fitted properly inside of God's story of redemption, is an event of great hope. In fact, it is the most hopeful thing that ever happened to us because God's story is the story that orders every event of our own lives.

1) What advice might the Chinese farmer give to the Emmaus travelers?

____

____

____

2) The gospel is called the "good news", which tells people of the salvation Jesus has given us. Although we should not judge hastily, we must still make judgments. Why is the farmer's refrain of "good news, bad news, who can say?" not a proper response to the gospel?

____

____

____

PART II: Furthering Your Knowledge

Remembering the importance of making wise judgments that agree with God's whole story, read the following passage about how God through Christ creates, sustains, and purposes creation. Read the left column if you want something more difficult or the right column for something easier.

---

1. Luke 24:21.
2. Luke 24:25-27.

As you read, underline parts you would like to ask questions about. Then use the lines at the end of this reading to write down any questions you might have for your teacher.

All Things Find their Purpose in the Person of Christ

Difficult	Simplified
(1) The theologian and philosopher Cornelius Van Til once wrote, "After his conversion he can't see a fact in the world that he does not wish to deal with to the glory of God."[3] He was speaking of the Christian's responsibility to interpret all of reality according to the God revealed in Scripture. Of course, the Bible isn't a physics textbook, for instance. However, it does tell us how we should understand physics, as well as every other field of study. Colossians 1:16 identifies Christ as the one through whom the entire universe is created, sustained, and purposed. Physics does not investigate a lifeless world, but explores the intricacies of Christ's magnificent creation. Even more, the mental faculties we use to carry out any scientific investigation also depend on Christ's work of creating and sustaining us. That is, "In him we live and move and have our being."[4] Everything we do, is made possible by Christ.	(1) The theologian and philosopher Cornelius Van Til wrote about Christians like this. "After his conversion he can't see a fact in the world that he does not wish to deal with to the glory of God."[3] He was saying that the Christian must interpret everything according to the God of the Bible. Of course, the Bible isn't a physics textbook, but it does tell us how to understand physics, as well as every other field of study. Colossians 1:16 says that the entire universe is created, supported, and purposed through Christ. Physics does not study a lifeless world, but looks at the details of Christ's wonderful creation. Even more, the minds we use for studying science also depend on Christ who made and supports us. "In him we live and move and have our being."[4]

3. Greg Bahnsen, *Van Til's Apologetic: Readings and Analysis* (Philipsburg, NJ: P and R Publishing Company, 1998), 93.
4. Acts 17:28.

(2) And what is true of us is also true of everything else in the universe. It all exists by the will and work of Christ. Quite simply, "All things were made through him, and without him was not any thing made that was made."[5] To quote Lesslie Newbigin, "...the ultimate reality which lies behind all our experience is, in some sense, personal."[6] Reality is not built upon principles such as scientific laws. Instead, reality is built upon a person, namely Jesus Christ. But these principles do direct us to this person. The laws of nature show us the order that Christ has given to his creation. Accordingly, Abraham Kuyper describes these as "...not laws originating *from* nature, but laws imposed *upon* Nature."[7] Of course, they have been imposed by Jesus Christ.	(2) And what is true of us is also true of everything else in the universe. It is all there by the will and work of Christ. Quite simply, "All things were made through him, and without him was not anything made that was made."[5] To quote Lesslie Newbigin, "...the ultimate reality which lies behind all our experience is, in some sense, personal."[6] When we ask, "Is this real?" we don't turn to the laws of science. Instead, we turn to a person, Jesus Christ. But the laws do direct us to this person. The laws of nature show us the order that Christ has given to his creation. Abraham Kuyper describes these as "...not laws originating *from* nature, but laws imposed *upon* Nature."[7] Of course, they have been put there by Jesus Christ.
(3) Our awe of Christ's relationship to his creation does not end here, though. That is, "...all things were created through and for him."[8] Not only did he create all things, but all things were also created for him. He is the purpose of all things.	(3) There is more to celebrate about Christ's relationship to his creation. That is, "...all things were created through and for him."[8] Here are two truths: he made all things, and all things were also made for him. He is the purpose of all things.

5. John 1:3.

6. Lesslie Newbigen, *The Gospel in a Pluralistic Society* (Grand Rapids, MI: Eerdmans, 1989), 61. This quote appears as a premise in an argument he puts forth. Since he affirms this premise the conditional "if" has been removed from the above quotation.

7. Abraham Kuyper, *Lectures on Calvinism* (Grand Rapids, MI: Eerdmans, 1931), 62.

8. Colossians 1:16.

(4) A creation with a purpose is what we should expect if God through Christ created and continually sustains his creation. As B.B. Warfield wrote, "That God acts upon a plan in all his activities, is already given in Theism...For person means purpose..."[9] Warfield goes on to explain that every choice a person makes is meant to accomplish some end or goal. In the same way, every act of God through Christ works to accomplish his purpose for the entire universe.	(4) A creation which has a purpose is not surprising if God through Christ created and always supports his creation. As B.B. Warfield wrote, "That God acts upon a plan in all his activities, is already given in Theism...For person means purpose..."[9] Then Warfield explains that every choice a person makes has a purpose. In the same way, every act of God through Christ works towards his purpose for the entire universe.
(5) Colossians does not keep us guessing about this purpose. God through Christ purposes "...to reconcile to himself all things, whether on earth or in heaven, making peace by the blood of his cross."[10] Warfield expressed this purpose in a similar way. Describing the fulfillment of God's plan, he wrote, "And as, when Christ comes, we shall each of us be like him, when we shall see him as he is, so also, when Christ comes, it will be to a fully saved world, and there shall be a new heaven and a new earth, in which dwells righteousness."[11] The whole world, the entire universe, will be made right. Not only we who are in Christ will be transformed, but also the universe that is created, sustained, and purposed through Christ.	(5) Colossians does not keep us guessing about this purpose. God through Christ wants "...to reconcile to himself all things, whether on earth or in heaven, making peace by the blood of his cross."[10] Warfield expressed this purpose like this, too. Here is what he wrote about God's plan and how it works out. "And as, when Christ comes, we shall each of us be like him, when we shall see him as he is, so also, when Christ comes, it will be to a fully saved world, and there shall be a new heaven and a new earth, in which dwells righteousness."[11] The whole world, the whole universe, will become right. Who will be changed? Not just Christians, but also the universe that is created, sustained, and purposed through Christ.

9. B.B. Warfield, *The Plan of Salvation: Five Lectures delivered at Princeton School of Theology: June, 1914* (Philadelphia: Presbyterian Board of Publication, 1915), 12.

10. Colossians 1:20.

11. Warfield, *The Plan of Salvation*, 130.

Notes/Questions

____

____

____

____

____

Vocabulary Focus: Word Forms[12]

For each sentence fill in the blank with the correct form of the word. Identify the part of speech (noun, verb, adjective, adverb) and fill in the blank on the right.

<u>Example</u>

He was speaking of the Christian's responsibility to <u>interpret</u> all of reality according to the God revealed in Scripture.	(interpret, interpreting, interpretation)	<u>verb</u>
1) God through Christ creates, sustains, and ____________ the entire universe.	(purposes, purposeful, purposely)	________
2) Physics explores the intricacies of Christ's ____________ creation.	(magnificence, magnificent, magnificently)	________
3) The laws of nature have been ____________ by Jesus Christ.	(impose, imposed, imposing)	________
4) Christ ____________ sustains his creation.	(continue, continues, continually)	________
5) All things were ____________ through him and for him.	(create, created, creating)	________
6) The ____________ of God's plan comes through Christ Jesus.	(fulfill, fulfilled, fulfillment)	________
7) We who are in Christ will be ____________.	(transform, transformed, transformation)	________
8) There shall be a new heaven and a new earth in which dwells ____________.	(righteous, righteously, righteousness)	________

12. For this section, you can check your work with the Answer Key found in the back of this book.

Think More About the Meaning

1) In paragraph 5, the article uses three verbs to express Christ's actions toward his creation: *create*, *sustain*, and *purpose*. In your own words, describe the importance of each statement.

   God through Christ creates his creation:

   God through Christ sustains his creation:

   God through Christ purposes his creation:

2) Does the article change the way you think about the world around you? Why or why not?

3) According to the article, what is the conclusion of Christ's story that allows us to properly interpret all the events of our life?

4) In Romans, Paul writes, "And we know that for those who love God all things work together for good, for those who are called according to his purpose." Does this passage agree with the parable about the farmer? Why or why not?

5) How does this passage relate to the theological article above?

____

____

____

PART II: A Parable of Jesus

Before Reading Consider...

Jesus tells his audience this parable "...to the effect that they ought always to pray and not lose heart".[13]

Keeping this purpose in mind, let's examine how Kevin Vanhoozer identifies four important aspects of biblical interpretation.[14] Interpretation is a process that readers work through in order understand what they are reading.

These four aspects that guide interpretation are described in the charts below: 1) propositional reference, 2) poetic form, 3) pedagogical nature and function, and 4) testimony to Jesus Christ. The third aspect deals specifically with Jesus' pedagogical purpose in telling the parable.

After you read the parable, work through the four charts. Each chart corresponds to Vanhoozer's four interpretive aspects and will help you think through the purpose of this passage.

The Parable of the Persistent Widow

He said, "In a certain city there was a judge who neither feared God nor respected man. And there was a widow in that city who kept coming to him and saying, 'Give me justice against my adversary.' For a while he refused, but afterward he said to himself, 'Though I neither fear God nor respect man, yet because this widow keeps bothering me, I will give her justice, so that she will not beat me down by her continual coming.'" And the Lord said, "Hear what the unrighteous judge says. And will not God give justice to his elect, who cry to him day and night? Will he delay long over them? I tell you, he will give justice to them speedily. Nevertheless, when the Son of Man comes, will he find faith on earth?"

(Luke 18:1-8)

13. Luke 18:1.

14. Kevin Vanhoozer, *Is There a Meaning in this Text?: The Bible, the Reader, and the Morality of Literary Knowledge* (Grand Rapids, MI: Zondervan, 1998), 312-313.

On the chart read the explanation of Vanhoozer's four aspects of biblical texts that guide interpretation. Then complete the corresponding exercises. Once you have completed the charts divide into four groups and discuss each aspect of Vanhoozer's model.

❶ *Propositional Reference*

Explanation

a) This interpretative aspect examines the objects and concepts that the words of a passage directly refer to. In the case of a parable, this aspect explores the actual story told and not the deeper meaning to which the story points.

Exercise

a) Summarize the story of the parable.

Explanation

b) Understanding the meaning of key words in the parable helps readers interpret its meaning.

Exercise

b) The phrase "beat down" literally translates into "give someone a black eye."[15]

Why do you think the parable uses this kind of violent imagery?

Do you have a word or phrase in your local language that can be used in a similar way? If so, explain.

15. Darrell L. Bock, *Luke: 9:51-24:53. Baker Exegetical Commentary on the New Testament*, Series, ed. Moises Silva. (Grand Rapids, MI: Baker Books, 1994), 1449.

❷ *Poetic Form*

Explanation

a) This interpretative aspect examines the literary form of a passage. The Bible has many literary forms, including poems, historical writings, and letters. Since we are focusing on parables, we need to know the literary conventions, or rules, that parables follow. These will help us interpret parables in the way that Jesus intended.

Exercise

a) The parable principles presented in each chapter of this textbook will aid your interpretation of parables. What is one particular principle, that you have studied so far, that will help you interpret this parable? Explain why.

Explanation

b) The parable of the persistent widow is an example of a "how much more" parable.[16] This type reasons from the lesser to the greater. It shows that if humans (the lesser) do something, then God (the greater) will certainly do it to a much greater degree. In this present case, "If an unjust judge will finally grant justice, how much more will God!"[17] Other parables of this type include the parables of the lost sheep (Luke 15:3-7)[18], the lost coin (Luke 15:8-10)[19], and the friend at midnight (Luke 11:5-8)[20]. This kind of parable reveals God through a kind of narrative analogy (or parallel story). This is an especially significant form of revelation because being "...created in God's image, humankind can be described as an analogy of God: similar but never the same."[21]

---

16. Snodgrass, *Stories with Intent*, 15.
17. Green, *The Gospel of Luke*, 452.
18. Ibid., 107.
19. Ibid., 112-113.
20. Ibid., 437.
21. Horton, *Introducing Covenant Theology*, 21-22.

Exercise

b) Thinking about the comparison between God and the unjust judge, complete the following exercise. Write a sentence describing the unjust judge and then a contrasting sentence describing God. Then combine these sentences with a suitable conjunction (whereas, while, although).

Example

Sentence 1: The unjust judge refuses to act justly.

Sentence 2: God must act justly because he cannot act against his just nature.

Combined Sentence with a conjunction: Whereas the unjust judge refuses to act justly, God must act justly because he cannot act against his just nature.

First Comparison[23]

Sentence 1:

Sentence 2:

Combine the two sentences with a conjunction:

Second Comparison

Sentence 1:

Sentence 2:

Combine the two sentences with a conjunction:

With these comparisons in mind, why do you think the narrative analogy between the unjust judge and God is a powerful way to express the surety of God's justice?

22. For this section, you can check your work with the Answer Key found in the back of this book.

❸ *Pedagogical Nature and Function (The Teaching Aspect)*

Explanation

a) This interpretive aspect examines what a passage teaches the church.

In this parable, Jesus has told the listeners the pedagogical purpose: "…that they ought always to pray and not lose heart."

Exercise

a) How does this parable fulfill the purpose of teaching the disciples to always pray and not lose heart?

Explanation

b) How does this passage of Scripture interact with the rest of Scripture?

As Vanhoozer writes, "What I have in mind is the Bible's character as 'Scripture' and 'canon'—its nature as a guidebook for the believing community."[23] In the case of this parable, Jesus' pedagogical purpose is: "…that they ought always to pray and not lose heart." Other Scriptures, which further reveal why we should pray and not lose heart, reinforce this purpose.

Exercise

b) What is another passage from the gospel of Luke that provides further insight into this purpose?

23. Vanhoozer, *Is There a Meaning in this Text?*, 313.

Explanation

c) Vanhoozer describes the church as a "living commentary"[24] of the Word of God. This means that one important way we can show how we understand Scripture is how we live out its teaching.

Exercise

c) Think of an unjust situation that you have recently heard about or experienced. Think of one way you could be a "living commentary" of this parable in that situation.

Now think about the Chinese parable. How could you be a "living commentary" of that parable in the unjust situation you considered above?

24. Ibid., 441.

❹ *Testimony to Jesus Christ*

Explanation

This interpretative aspect examines what a passage reveals about Christ and how this revelation forms part of the Bible's unified witness of Christ.

Revealing Christ is Scripture's ultimate purpose. For instance, the article in chapter 4 about typology shows one way that the Old Testament testifies to the person and work of Christ.

Exercise

Read the following passage for the main idea. Underline or highlight key words or phrases.

Our Eschatological Assurance in Christ:

(1) In showing the kingdom of God, the parables have an eschatological significance. That is, they reveal to us what will happen when the kingdom of God comes in all its fullness and the current age is ended. Chapter 4 discussed the "already but not yet" of the kingdom, but eschatology tells of when the kingdom's "not yet" dynamic is no more. Christ's return will mark the full arrival of the kingdom of God to earth, the fulfillment of his purpose for all of creation.

2) Jesus closes the present parable by calling us to eschatological assurance. He says, "And will not God give justice to his elect, who cry to him day and night? Will he delay long over them? I tell you, he will give justice to them speedily. Nevertheless, when the Son of Man comes, will he find faith on earth?" Because God's justice for his people is certain, Jesus implies that there is no reason why they should ever lack faith in his purposes, no matter what hardships they face. Christ will vindicate them by punishing all injustice.

(3) But here, again, we find the "already but not yet" dynamic of the kingdom of God. As Klyne Snodgrass writes about this parable, "Vindication has begun with the kingdom and the resurrection of Jesus, but it awaits God's future eschatological action."[25] He cites Revelation 6:10[26] as a passage that helps us better understand this parable because it shows Christ's concern for "his elect, who cry to him day and night." In this verse, the martyrs of the church, those who have experienced a very severe injustice, cry out saying, "O Sovereign Lord, holy and true, how long before you will judge and avenge our blood on those who dwell on the earth?" At present, Christ has vindicated both them and us in part, but soon, he will vindicate us all in full.

25. Snodgrass, *Stories with Intent*, 462.

26. Ibid., 456.

Summarize each of the above paragraphs in one sentence. An example has been provided for paragraph 1.

Paragraph 1[27]

Parables can hold an eschatological significance that tells us what will happen when Christ returns and the kingdom of God fully arrives on Earth.

Paragraph 2

Paragraph 3

Look over your three summary sentences. What do they communicate about Christ's person and work?

Think of at least two ways that your summaries relate to the theological article in this chapter that describes how Christ creates, sustains, and purposes all of creation.

27. For this section, you can check your work with the Answer Key found in the back of this book.

PART IV: Writing Your Own Parable

Parable Principle 5
Parables frequently have a purpose of concealing, as well as revealing.[28] An audience often needs additional explanation to grasp the intended meaning of the parable. In such cases, the story alone is not enough for adequate understanding.

We see this need for explanation in the parable of the sower. After telling the parable, the disciples ask Jesus about its meaning. He answers, "To you it has been given to know the secrets of the kingdom of God, but for others they are in parables, so that 'seeing they may not see, and hearing they may not understand.'"[29] Jesus then explains the parable to his disciples point by point.

When we think of this in light of the interpretation process above, we can find a link between this concealing and the need to understand each part of Scripture in light of the whole of Scripture. For instance, none of Jesus' parables can stand alone. Instead, we must interpret each parable within the whole of Scripture. Knowing the whole helps us understand each part. At the same time, each parable contributes to this unified testimony. So we better understand each part (e.g., each parable) through our understanding of the whole (all of Scripture), and we better understand the whole through our understanding of each part. This dynamic process forms the basic pattern of what has been called the hermeneutical circle.

1) How did working through the stages of interpretation help you understand the parable of the persistent widow in light of other passages and the whole message of Scripture?

___

___

___

2) How does this process of interpretation relate to the section above that explains how each individual event must be interpreted according to the whole of Scripture?

___

___

___

28. Blomberg, *Interpreting the Parables*, 65.

29. Luke 8:10.

Christ says, "...the Holy Spirit, whom the Father will send in my name, he will teach you all things and bring to your remembrance all that I have said to you."[30] Vanhoozer puts it as follows, "The Holy Spirit is the Spirit of the Word—the Spirit of Christ—and ministers Christ, the matter of Scripture, to its readers."[31] Or as he says elsewhere, "The Spirit ministers the word that communicates Christ, the word that relates us to Christ, the word that enables communion with Christ."[32] The Spirit ensures that God's Word accomplishes its purpose as it is read by those to whom "...it has been given to know the secrets of the kingdom of God." In turn, to properly understand the parables and the king and kingdom they reveal, we need the hermeneutical work of the Holy Spirit.

3) Is this an activity you regularly associate with the Holy Spirit? Why or why not?

____

____

____

____

Think about the parable you are writing. What are some Scripture passages that directly relate to your parable's meaning? Fill in the chart below listing the passages and briefly explaining their relations to your parable.

Passage	Relation

30. John 14:25-26.
31. Vanhoozer, *Is There a Meaning in This Text?*, 429.
32. Vanhoozer, *The Drama of Doctrine*, 208.

The Holy Spirit is active whenever Christ is preached. Preaching Christ is what you intend to do with your parable. Reflect on what you hope the Spirit does in the hearts and minds of your audience through your parable. Below, write a prayer that expresses these hopes.

6

Expecting the Exalted King

In this chapter you will read a parable that shows the dangers of mistaken expectations. Then you will learn about the ways that Jesus countered the expectations that his contemporaries held about his kingship and kingdom. Through it all, you will reflect on how Jesus' person and work are much greater than any of the presumptions he confronted then and still confronts now.

PART I: Halcolm's Parable

Before Reading Consider...

- What is something that you have studied about but never seen or experienced firsthand?
- Why does this thing interest you?
- What would it be like to see or experience this thing firsthand?

The Scholar and the Fruit
By M.Q. Patton (Halcolm's Inquiry Parables)[1]

(1) There once lived a man in a country with no fruit trees. A scholar, he spent a great deal of time reading. He often came across references to fruit. The descriptions enticed him to undertake a journey to experience fruit for himself.

(2) He went to the marketplace and inquired where he could find the land of fruit. After much searching he located someone who knew the way. After a long and arduous

1. Michael Quinn Patton, *Qualitative Evaluation and Research Methods 3rd Edition* (Newbury, CA: Sage Publications, 2002), 3.

journey, he came to the end of the directions and found himself at the entrance to a large apple orchard. It was springtime and the apple trees were in blossom.

(3) The scholar entered the orchard and, expectantly, pulled off a blossom and put it in his mouth. He liked neither the texture of the flower nor its taste. He went quickly to another tree and sampled another blossom, and then another, and another. Each blossom, though quite beautiful, was distasteful to him. He left the orchard and returned to his home country, reporting to his fellow villagers that fruit was a much-overrated food.

(4) Being unable to recognize the difference between the spring blossom and the summer fruit, the scholar never realized that he had not experienced what he was looking for.

Notes/Questions

____

____

____

____

____

Theological Connection

1) Why do you think the scholar mistook the blossoms for apples?

____

____

____

2) If you had been able to speak with the scholar before his journey to the land of fruit, what advice would you have given him? Imagine that you have never seen fruit either and tell him how he should plan his investigation.

____

____

____

3) In John 5:39-40, Jesus tells an angry crowd, "You search the Scriptures because you think that in them you have eternal life; and it is they that bear witness about me, yet you refuse to come to me that you may have life." Despite their rigorous study of

the Old Testament, Jesus' Jewish audience does not realize that these writings testify about him. How is this similar to the scholar's mistake as described in the parable?

____

____

____

PART II: Furthering Your Knowledge

There are many ways that Jesus contradicted the expectations of his Jewish audience. Read the following passage about the astonishing nature of Jesus' kingship. Read the left column if you want something more difficult or the right column for something easier. To ease your reading, the article has been divided into two parts.

As you read, underline parts you would like to ask questions about. Use the lines at the end of this reading to write down any questions you might have for your teacher.

The Son of God and the Son of David (Part 1)

Difficult	Simplified
(1) The gospel according to Luke announces that Jesus is the long awaited king in the line of David. In fact, many of the events surrounding the life of Jesus, which Luke recounts, parallel events that establish David's kingship. As N.T. Wright explains, "Luke is telling the story of Jesus as the fulfillment, the completion, of the story of David and his kingdom."[2] In particular, Wright points out how Luke's opening chapters correspond with many happenings in the book of 1 Samuel.[3]	(1) In the book of Luke we read that Jesus is the expected king descended from David. He is the one everyone was waiting for. Many things about the life of Jesus, as told in the book of Luke, are similar to things that made David king. As N.T. Wright says, "Luke is telling the story of Jesus as the fulfillment, the completion, of the story of David and his kingdom."[2] Wright shows how Luke's opening chapters are like a mirror of many happenings in the book of 1 Samuel.[3]

2. Wright, *The New Testament and the People of God*, 381.
3. Ibid., 378-380. The examples in the next paragraph are taken from Wright's explanation.

(2) The childlessness of Zechariah and Elizabeth reminds readers of Hannah and Elkanah's longing for a child.[4] Both couples receive a son from the Lord with Elizabeth bearing John the Baptist and Hannah bearing Samuel. When they reach adulthood, John and Samuel both pronounce God's judgment on the people of Israel, but they also announce God's coming deliverance. That is, the highest point in their respective ministries is their anointing of God's true king. Samuel anoints David as Israel's king, "And the Spirit of the Lord rushed upon David from that day forward."[5] Then, many years later, John anoints Jesus through baptism, after which the heavens open and the same Spirit that rushed upon David descends on Jesus in the form of a dove.

(2) Zechariah and Elizabeth had no children, which reminds us of how Hannah and Elkanah also wanted a child.[4] Both couples receive a son from the Lord. Elizabeth had John the Baptist and Hannah had Samuel. As adults, John and Samuel both tell about God's judgment on the people of Israel, but they also tell about God's coming deliverance. That is, the greatest part of both of their ministries is that they anointed God's true king. Samuel anoints David as Israel's king. "And the Spirit of the Lord rushed upon David from that day forward."[5] Then, many years later, John baptizes Jesus. After he does that, the heavens open and the same Spirit that came down to David comes down on Jesus like a dove.

(3) From there, God the Father proclaims to Jesus, "You are my beloved Son; with you I am well pleased."[6] This proclamation, which was heard by the crowd gathered around John the Baptist, is a fulfillment of a long awaited expectation. In 2 Samuel 7, God promises David, "When your days are fulfilled and you lie down with your fathers, I will raise up your offspring after you, who shall come from your body, and I will establish his kingdom. He shall build a house for my name, and I will establish the throne of his kingdom forever. I will be to him a father, and he shall be to me a son."[7]

(3) Then God the Father says to Jesus, "You are my beloved Son; with you I am well pleased."[6] These words were heard by the crowd gathered around John the Baptist. They showed that Jesus was the fulfillment of a promise that had been made to David long ago. In 2 Samuel 7, God promises David, "When your days are fulfilled and you lie down with your fathers, I will raise up your offspring after you, who shall come from your body, and I will establish his kingdom. He shall build a house for my name, and I will establish the throne of his kingdom forever. I will be to him a father, and he shall be to me a son."[7]

4. 1 Samuel 1.

5. 1 Samuel 16:13.

6. Luke 3:22.

7. 2 Samuel 7:12-14.

The immediate fulfillment of God's promise to David was the kingship of his son Solomon, but its complete fulfillment is found later in David's lineage in Jesus. He is the Son of God who reigns forever, the Son with whom the Father is well pleased.

God's promise to David came true in part when his son Solomon became king. It came true completely with Jesus' kingship. He is the Son of God who reigns forever, the Son with whom the Father is well pleased.

(4) Immediately after Jesus' baptism, Luke goes on to stress the two-fold identity of Jesus. As the Christ, he is both the Son of God and the son of David, both fully God and fully man. And so Luke devotes the rest of chapter 3 to tracing Jesus' ancestry back to David and back further still to its very beginning. The last link in this messianic family line tells us that Jesus is the Son of God.[8]

(4) Immediately after Jesus' baptism, Luke tells us more about who Jesus is. As the Christ, he is the Son of God and the son of David, both fully God and fully man. And so, in the rest of chapter 3, Luke shows how Jesus' family goes back to David and back further still to its very beginning. The last part of this messianic family line tells us that Jesus is the Son of God.[8]

(5) However, the first part of Luke's fourth chapter recounts Satan's tempting of Jesus, temptations that also address Jesus' divine sonship. Of the three temptations that Satan puts to Jesus, both the first and third begin with the conditional clause, "If you are the Son of God..." It appears that Satan attempted to compromise the person and work of Jesus by questioning his divine sonship. Perhaps Satan thought it possible to make Jesus doubt that he was the Son of God. But Christ, of course, was not shaken.

(5) However, the first part of Luke's fourth chapter tells how Satan tempted Jesus. This story also tells us that Jesus is the Son of God. Satan puts three temptations to Jesus. The first and third begin with these words, "If you are the Son of God..." It looks as if Satan tried to attack the person and work of Jesus by asking a question. Was Jesus really the Son of God? Perhaps Satan thought he could make Jesus ask that question. But Christ, of course, did not doubt that he was the Son of God.

8. Luke 3:38.

Notes/Questions

____

____

____

____

____

____

____

____

____

Vocabulary Focus[9]

Read the sentences below and use the context to identify the part of speech and to understand the meaning of the word in bold. Write the part of speech (noun, adjective, verb, adverb) in the parentheses and the definition in the blank. Check your answers with a partner.

Example

The **childlessness** of Zechariah and Elizabeth reminds readers of Hannah and Elkanah's longing for a child.

childlessness (*noun*): a state of being without children. Zechariah and Elizabeth cannot have children.

1) The gospel according to Luke **announces** that Jesus is the long awaited king in the line of David.

   announces (   ):

   ____

   ____

2) The Spirit of the Lord **rushed upon** David from that day forward.

   rushed upon (   ):

   ____

   ____

9. For this section, you can check your work with the Answer Key found in the back of this book.

3) I will raise up your **offspring** after you, who shall come from your body…

offspring ( ):

---

4) The immediate **fulfillment** of God's promise to David was the kingship of his son Solomon...

fulfillment ( ):

---

5) Its complete fulfillment is found later in David's **lineage** in Jesus.

lineage ( ):

---

6) The first part of Luke's fourth chapter **recounts** Satan's tempting Jesus…

recounts ( ):

---

7) It appears that Satan attempted to **compromise** the person and work of Jesus by questioning his **divine** sonship.

compromise ( ):

---

divine ( ):

Vocabulary Strategy: Identifying Noun Suffixes in Context[10]

Suffixes are word endings that change the meaning of a word. Some common noun suffixes are: *-ion*/*-tion*/*-ation*, *-ship*, *-ment*, *-ism*, and *-ness*. Read the passage (*The Son of God and the Son of David: Part 1*) carefully and circle the nouns with these suffixes. Complete the chart. There are other noun suffixes that have a different ending. Place these words in

10. For this section, you can check your work with the Answer Key found in the back of this book.

the "other" category on the chart. Examples have been provided. Discuss your answers with a partner.

-ion/-tion/ -ation	-ship	-ment	-ness	other suffix ending
presentation	friendship	entertainment	righteousness	theology

Next, choose one noun from each category on the chart and write a sentence.

Example
–ion/tion/ation: She gave a presentation at the theological conference.

1) –ion/tion/ation: ______________________________________

2) –ship: ____

3) –ment: ____

4) –ness: ____

5) –other suffix ending: ____________________________________

Think More About the Meaning

1) The first part of this article identified a number of parallel events in the lives of Samuel and John the Baptist. Use the table below to compare and contrast these life events.

Similarities between their lives	Differences between their lives

2) How does the article relate to the article in chapter 4 about typology? What office of Christ does this article highlight and why?

____

____

____

3) Review the explanation of the *Testimony to Jesus of Christ* on page 93. Choose one of the Old Testament passages referenced in the first part of this chapter's article and explain how it testifies to Christ.

____

____

____

As you read the following section, underline parts you would like to ask questions about. Use the lines at the end of this reading to write down any questions you might have for your teacher.

The Son of God and the Son of David (Part 2)

Difficult	Simplified
(1) Others were shaken though, as the inauguration of Jesus' kingship on earth looked very different than what anyone had expected. Even John the Baptist began to have doubts about Jesus' identity, asking, "Are you the one who is to come, or shall we look for another?"[11] Then, contrary to all messianic expectations, Jesus' kingship was mocked publicly. He suffered the shameful death of crucifixion wearing a crown not of gold, but of thorns, underneath a sign that read, "This is the King of the Jews,"[12] not in sincerity, but in satire.	(1) Others did doubt though because Jesus' life looked very different from what anyone was expecting. Even John the Baptist began to have doubts about who Jesus was. He asked, "Are you the one who is to come, or shall we look for another?"[11] Then, against all expectations for the Messiah, people publicly made fun of Jesus the king. He suffered the shameful death of crucifixion wearing a crown not of gold, but of thorns, underneath a sign that read, "This is the King of the Jews."[12] The people who wrote these words did not believe them. The words were meant to mock Jesus.
(2) However, Jesus' most painful suffering came not from human hands but from God his Father. In complete contrast to when the heavens opened and God the Father declared Jesus' divine sonship, the sky was darkened while he hung on the cross.[13] Even more, no voice from heaven was there to answer his cry of "My God, my God, why have you forsaken me?"[14] God his Father had rejected him. But this rejection is the greatest act of love the world has ever known. We were the ones who deserved that rejection of sonship. But Jesus took our place. He endured the silence of the heavens so that we could receive the declaration that only he deserves:	(2) However, Jesus' worst suffering came not from people but from God his Father. This time the heavens did not open and there was no voice from God telling people that Jesus was his Son. Instead, the sky darkened while he was on the cross.[13] Even more, God did not answer his cry of "My God, my God, why have you forsaken me?"[14] God his Father had turned away from him. But this turning away shows the greatest love the world has even known. We deserved to be told we were not God's sons but Jesus took our place. He suffered the silence of the heavens so we could receive the words that only he deserves:

11. Luke 7:19
12. Luke 23:38.
13. Matthew 27:45.
14. Matthew 27:37.

"You are my beloved Son; with you I am well pleased."[15] As John the apostle would go on to write, "See what kind of love the Father has given to us, that we should be called children of God; and so we are."[16]

(3) Paul reinforces this reality by showing how the same Spirit that anointed Christ and David is at work in us. He writes, "The Spirit himself bears witness with our spirit that we are children of God, and if children, then heirs—heirs of God and fellow heirs with Christ..."[17] And of course, we are not co-heirs with a dead king. That would be impossible. In the introduction of Romans, Paul declares the resurrection of the Christ, the king who lives and reigns forever. He brings together the Messiah's kingship and divine sonship, writing that Jesus Christ is the one, "...who was descended from David according to the flesh and was declared to be the Son of God in power according to the Spirit of holiness by his resurrection from the dead, Jesus Christ our Lord..."[18] Even more, Paul is pointing out that Jesus' death gave God the Father, through the Spirit, the most powerful opportunity to declare Jesus' divine sonship. Jesus' resurrection from the dead is a declaration to all that he is the Son of God and, therefore, the true king of the world.

"You are my beloved Son; with you I am well pleased."[15] As John the apostle later wrote, "See how much love the Father has given to us, by calling us children of God; and so we are."[16]

(3) Paul shows this is true. He says that the same Spirit that anointed Christ and David works in us. He writes, "The Spirit himself bears witness with our spirit that we are children of God, and if children, then heirs—heirs of God and fellow heirs with Christ..."[17] And of course, we are not co-heirs with a dead king. That would be impossible. At the beginning of Romans, Paul talks about the resurrection of the Christ, the king who lives and reigns forever. He ties it all together writing that Jesus is the one, "...who was descended from David according to the flesh and was declared to be the Son of God in power according to the Spirit of holiness by his resurrection from the dead, Jesus Christ our Lord..."[18] Even more, Paul is saying that Jesus' death gave God the Father, through the Spirit, the greatest chance to demonstrate that Jesus is the son of God. Jesus' rising from the dead shows everyone that he is God's son and, therefore, the true king of the world.

15. In Christ, there are both sons and daughters of God, but here, for exegetical purposes, it is important to focus on "sonship" because of the status it implied in that culture. In the same way, Christian males should not refuse the label of the church as "the bride of Christ." These terms have implications that transcend, or go beyond, the gender of any particular Christian.

16. 1 John 3:1.

17. Romans 8:16-17.

18. Romans 1:3-4.

Notes/Questions

Think More About the Meaning

1) Think again about how Jesus answered an angry Jewish crowd in John 5:39-40. He said, "You search the Scriptures because you think that in them you have eternal life; and it is they that bear witness about me, yet you refuse to come to me that you may have life." Why do you think the people in Jesus' day did not see him as the fulfillment of God's covenant of kingship with David?

2) Christ was rejected so that we could be accepted as children of God and co-heirs with Christ the king. Paul often refers to this process as adoption. And, as J. Todd Billings writes, "We need not only adoption into God's family and forgiveness of sins; we need also to learn how to grow into our new identity as adopted children of the Triune God."[19] As you think about this quote, review the section about justification and sanctification in chapter 1.

   As the following diagram illustrates, Billings connects justification with the first clause of the sentence quoted above and sanctification with the second clause.

19. J. Todd Billings, *Union with Christ: Reframing Theology and Ministry for the Church* (Grand Rapids, MI: Baker Academic, 2011), 29.

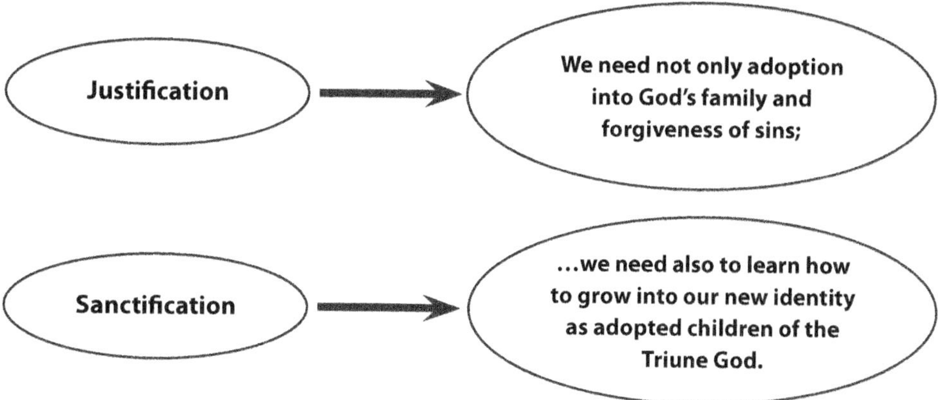

How does conceptualizing justification and sanctification in terms of adoption into the royal family of God affect your understanding of these theological terms?

____

____

____

____

____

3) Read the following excerpt from John Frame regarding the use of metaphor in theology.

> In God's world, everything is, after all, comparable to everything else. Granted, we tend to wince a bit when something we love or admire is compared to what we consider an unworthy object. But remember, Scripture even compares God to an unjust judge. Everything is related to everything else. There is nothing that "has nothing to do with" anything else . . . If someone compares God to a watermelon, for example, that fact is of little interest. What is of interest is what that metaphor is used to say about God. (If someone uses it to say that God's attributes, like the seeds of the watermelon, can be removed from him, he is telling a lie about God. If he uses it to describe the "sweetness" of our fellowship with God, he is telling the truth.)[20]

20. Frame, *The Doctrine of the Knowledge of God*, 231-232.

Reflecting on the two parts of the article and Frame's passage, use a metaphor to compare Jesus to the apples that were passed over by the scholar in the parable of the scholar and the fruit.

____

____

____

____

Vocabulary Focus[21]

Look up each word in your dictionary. Identify the part of speech (noun, adjective, verb, adverb). Write a short definition that is appropriate for the word as it is used below.

<u>*Example*</u>

rejected — God his Father had rejected him.

<u>verb</u> (part of speech) — <u>to refuse to believe, accept or consider someone or something</u> (definition)

1) pronounce — When they reach adulthood, John and Samuel both pronounce God's judgment on the people of Israel.

__________ (part of speech) — ____________________ (definition)

2) mocked — Jesus' kingship was mocked publicly.

__________ (part of speech) — ____________________ (definition)

3) messianic — The last link in this messianic family line tells us that Jesus is the Son of God.

__________ (part of speech) — ____________________ (definition)

21. For this section, you can check your work with the Answer Key found in the back of this book.

4) divine

It appears that Satan attempted to compromise the person and work of Jesus by questioning his divine sonship.

______________________ ____

(part of speech) (definition)

5) inauguration

The inauguration of Jesus' kingship on earth looked very different than what anyone expected.

______________________ ____

(part of speech) (definition)

6) rejection

But this rejection is the greatest act of love the world has ever known.

______________________ ____

(part of speech) (definition)

7) anointed

Paul reinforces this reality by showing how the same Spirit that anointed Christ and David is at work in us.

______________________ ____

(part of speech) (definition)

8) declaration

Jesus' resurrection from the dead was a declaration to all that he is the Son of God…

______________________ ____

(part of speech) (definition)

Grammar Focus: Noun Clauses[22]

A noun clause is a group of words that can be used in the same ways and in the same places as nouns in sentences. Noun clauses usually begin with *that* or question words like *who, whose, which, how, when.* Each of the sentences below has a noun clause. Underline the noun clause(s) in each sentence. There may be more than one noun clause in a sentence.

> *Example*
>
> David knew that he had sinned before God.

1) The gospel according to Luke announces that Jesus is the long awaited king in the line of David.

2) Many of the events surrounding the life of Jesus, which Luke recounts, parallel events that establish David's kingship.

3) Wright points out how Luke's opening chapters correspond with many happenings in the book of 1 Samuel.

4) The same Spirit that rushed upon David descends upon Jesus in the form of a dove.

5) I will raise up your offspring after you, who shall come from your body, and I will establish his kingdom.

6) The last link in the messianic family line tells us that Jesus is the Son of God.

7) Are you the one who is to come, or shall we look for another?

8) We are the ones who deserved that rejection of sonship.

PART III: A Parable of Jesus

Before Reading Consider...

As examined in chapter 5, Luke informed us of the pedagogical purpose (teaching point) of the parable of the persistent widow. In telling this parable, Jesus meant that his disciples "...ought always to pray and not lose heart." Similarly, Luke explains the mistake that

---

22. For this section, you can check your work with the Answer Key found in the back of this book.

Jesus intended to correct with the following parable. Luke prefaces the parable of the ten minas with, "As they heard these things, he proceeded to tell a parable, because he was near to Jerusalem, and because they supposed that the kingdom of God was to appear immediately. He said therefore…"

Reflecting on this mistaken expectation, what do you think is the pedagogical purpose of the following parable?

____

____

____

____

____

The Parable of the Ten Minas

As they heard these things, he proceeded to tell a parable, because he was near to Jerusalem, and because they supposed that the kingdom of God was to appear immediately. He said therefore, "A nobleman went into a far country to receive for himself a kingdom and then return. Calling ten of his servants, he gave them ten minas, and said to them, 'Engage in business until I come.' But his citizens hated him and sent a delegation after him, saying, 'We do not want this man to reign over us.' When he returned, having received the kingdom, he ordered these servants to whom he had given the money to be called to him, that he might know what they had gained by doing business. The first came before him, saying, 'Lord, your mina has made ten minas more.' And he said to him, 'Well done, good servant! Because you have been faithful in a very little, you shall have authority over ten cities.' And the second came, saying, 'Lord, your mina has made five minas.' And he said to him, 'And you are to be over five cities.' Then another came, saying, 'Lord, here is your mina, which I kept laid away in a handkerchief; for I was afraid of you, because you are a severe man. You take what you did not deposit, and reap what you did not sow.' He said to him, 'I will condemn you with your own words, you wicked servant! You knew that I was a severe man, taking what I did not deposit and reaping what I did not sow? Why then did you not put my money in the bank, and at my coming I might have collected it with interest?' And he said to those who stood by, 'Take the mina from him, and give it to the one who has the ten minas.' And they said to him, 'Lord, he has ten minas!' 'I tell you that to everyone who has, more will be given, but from the one who has not, even what he has will be taken away. But as for these enemies of mine, who did not want me to reign over them, bring them here and slaughter them before me.'"

(Luke 19:11-27)

Important Cultural Information

- A mina was roughly equal to the amount of money a common laborer would have earned for 100 days of work.[23]
- In this parable, Jesus alludes to the then recent situation of Archelaus, the son of Herod the Great, who traveled to Rome after his father's death to receive the right to be king over Judea. However, he was a very unpopular ruler. In fact, a delegation of Jews from Judea followed him to Rome to protest his kingship. Jesus intends for his audience to make connections between the nobleman of the parable and Archelaus.[24]

Fluency Practice: Put the Sentences of the Dialogue in Order[25]

Don't look at the parable above as you do this exercise. First, work in pairs or groups to put these sentences in the correct order. Number the sentences from 1-19. Number 1 has been done for you. Then count off around the class and read the sentences in order to reproduce the dialogue. If you have fewer than 19 people then take two numbers each.

Example

1 Everyone please work hard until I come back.

In pairs or small groups put the dialogue in order.

_____ Now, who's next?

_____ Just a minute. He already has ten minas!

_____ Lord, I have been careful with your money. Here is your one mina. I kept it safely in a handkerchief. Do you want to know why?

_____ Good. Now let me see the person over there. What happened to your money?

_____ I tell you that to everyone who has, more will be given, but from the one who has not even what he has will be taken away.

23. Snodgrass, *Stories with Intent*, 528.

24. The information from this paragraph is taken from Snodgrass, *Stories with Intent*, 537, and Wilcock, *The Savior of the World*, 173-174.

25. For this section, you can check your work with the Answer Key found in the back of this book.

_____ You did. Now listen everyone. Take the mina from this last man, and give it to the one who has the ten minas.

__1__ Everyone please work hard until I come back.

_____ I'm pleased with you. You can lead five cities. Third person, please.

_____ Lord, your one mina has made ten minas more.

_____ Yes. Why did you do that?

_____ Sorry but you have not done a good thing. If you knew that I was a severe man, taking what I did not deposit and reaping what I did not sow, then why then did you not put my money in the bank?

_____ That's great. You are a good servant! Because you have worked hard with only a little money I'll make you the leader of ten cities.

_____ I was afraid of you, because you are a severe man. You take what you did not deposit, and reap what you did not sow.

_____ Because then on my return I could have collected it with interest.

_____ It's me. Look, your one mina has made five minas.

_____ Why would I put it in the bank?

_____ Thank you. Off I go to lead ten cities.

_____ Now I'm back. Everyone who had money please come here.

_____ Oh dear. I did the wrong thing.

Examining the Parable

Michael Wilcock summarizes this parable as follows:

> The gist of the parable is that the nobleman is away long enough for his citizens to reveal their real enmity to him and for his servants to make full proof of their responsibilities to him. It is only after quite a long time that he returns in 'kingly power,' and then he settles with both groups.[26]

In the following boxes, you will connect this summary to details from the parable and then relate them to Christ's kingship.

a) ...the nobleman is away long enough for his citizens to reveal their real enmity to him...

The Nobleman's Journey Where did he go?   Why did he go there?

The Enmity of the Citizens How did the citizens feel about the nobleman?   How did they fight against the nobleman's kingship?

Connection to Christ's Kingship

We must never forget that Christ's parables reveal his kingship and kingdom. Like the surprising comparison with the unjust judge, this parable relates Christ's kingship to the unpopular reign of Archelaus. "In effect the parable charges that some Jews were resisting

26. Wilcock, *The Savior of the World*, 174.

the reign of the Messiah as if he were Archelaus."[27] With this in mind, let us address the above questions again in relation to Christ.

How did some of the Jews feel about Jesus?

____

____

____

How did they fight against Jesus' kingship?

____

____

____

b) ... and for his servants to make full proof of their responsibilities to him.

His Servants
How were the servants of the parable instructed to demonstrate their faithfulness to the nobleman while he was away?

Who was faithful and who was not?

Connection to Christ's Kingship

In Luke 6:45, Jesus tells a great multitude, "The good person out of the good treasure of his heart produces good, and the evil person out of his evil treasure produces evil, for out of the abundance of the heart his mouth speaks." Christ's true servants have hearts that love and rejoice in him. These faithful hearts naturally produce good works.

What do the words of the unfaithful servant show us about his heart and its relation to the nobleman?

____

____

____

27. Snodgrass, *Stories with Intent*, 537.

The ultimate cause of the servant's condemnation is his unfaithful heart. "That absence of faith is what Jesus condemns here, for it is that heart attitude that prevents this servant from pursuing the master's call."[28]

How did the actions of the servant, like his words, also demonstrate the condition of his heart?

____

____

____

____

c) It is only after quite a long time that he returns in "kingly power," and then he settles with both groups.

Settling with Both Groups

How does the nobleman settle the situation with the citizens?

How does he settle the situation with his servants?

Connection to Christ's Kingship

This "settling" happens after the nobleman returns in "kingly power." Christ told this parable to counter expectations "...that the kingdom of God was to appear immediately." Living in the "already but not yet" of the kingdom of God, we are also waiting for the return of Christ the king. And upon his return, he will likewise settle with two basic groups: those who hate him in their hearts and those who love him in their hearts. During this interim time, as in the parable, servants with faithful hearts will naturally produce good works.

28. Darrell L. Bock, *Luke: The NIV Application Commentary* (Grand Rapids, MI: Zondervan, 1996), 489.

Does the unfaithful servant ultimately belong with the group of rebellious citizens or with the group of faithful servants? Why?

How does the character of the unfaithful servant relate to persons who confess Christ with their mouths but reject him in their hearts?

The Judgment Christ Both Gives and Receives

(1) The parable ends with a strong example of the nobleman's judgment. He says, "But as for these enemies of mine, who did not want me to reign over them, bring them here and slaughter them before me." Klyne Snodgrass points out these strong words of judgment belong to the fictional character of the nobleman in the story and that they are not Jesus' clear teaching on judgment. Also, he explains that the language and details of parables are often exaggerated to catch people's attention. However, Snodgrass also warns us not to ignore the eschatological implication of the nobleman's judgment. We cannot forget that Jesus uses this parable as a way to teach us about his kingship and his kingdom. And certainly Jesus will return to judge the world.[29]

(2) However, Jesus' kingship goes against our expectations. Jesus is now exalted at the right hand of the Father and one day he will be exalted throughout the whole world as its true king. To be sure, Jesus' exaltation is much greater than his Jewish audience could have expected. But not only did their expectations of his kingship not account for the height of his exaltation, they also failed to account for the depth of his humiliation on the cross. And this humiliation must be kept in mind whenever we encounter passages of God's judgment. Regarding the present parable, Snodgrass says, "As Luke and his

29. Information from this paragraph taken from *Stories with Intent*, 540-541.

readers knew, rather than doing the slaughtering, Jesus is the one slaughtered. He is caught up in the judgment he announces, but there is still a day of reckoning."[30]

(3) On the cross, Jesus received the judgment that we deserve, "like a lamb that is led to the slaughter."[31] He took our sin so that we could be counted righteous before God. He was rejected by his Father so that we could be accepted as God's royal children. There will be a day when he returns to judge the world. However, for those who are in Christ, he has already suffered the judgment for them. That is, the cross has united God's love for his people and his judgment against their sin, showing God to be both perfectly loving and perfectly just. As D.A. Carson writes:

> "Do you wish to see God's love? Look at the cross.
> "Do you wish to see God's wrath? Look at the cross."[32]

Summarize each of three paragraphs above in one sentence.

1) ______________________________

____

____

2) ______________________________

____

____

3) ______________________________

____

____

---

30. Ibid., 541
31. Isaiah 53:7.
32. D.A. Carson, *The Difficult Doctrine of the Love of God* (Wheaton, IL: Crossway, 2000), 70-71.

Reflecting on your summaries, complete the following chart.

What are some examples of the humiliation Christ suffered to bring us into his kingdom?	What are some examples of Christ's present and future (eschatological) exaltation as king of the universe?

PART IV: Writing Your Own Parable

Parable Principle 6
Parables contain events common in the normal life of their audience. However, in order to call attention to their deeper meanings, parables usually communicate these events in exaggerated ways. These exaggerated elements will often seem improbable but, in Jesus' parables, they forcefully direct his audience to the truths of his kingdom.[33]

Both of the parables examined in this chapter address the dangers of incorrect expectations and they do so by describing realistic events in extraordinary ways. Halcolm's parable shows how our expectations can cause us to overlook the actual thing we are searching for. Jesus' parable countered the expectations of his audience by teaching them that his kingdom would not "appear immediately," but would arrive in fullness at a later date. Reflect on the ways that both parables exaggerate realistic events to better communicate their deeper meanings. Then do the exercise below.

The chart on the following page has been partially completed. Only fill in the four blank boxes.

33. Blomberg, *Interpreting the Parables*, 45-46.

Parable	Realistic Events	Exaggerated details of these events	Deeper meanings of these events
The Scholar and the Fruit	A scholar studies much about something and then goes to investigate the thing firsthand.		
The Ten Minas		The two faithful servants were given an extravagant reward. As many minas as they earned, they were put over that many cities. However, the nobleman's enemies received the extremely severe judgment of being slaughtered before him.	

Now think about the parable you are writing. Use the chart below to think how you might change the events of your parable in a way that exaggerates its details. Then explain how these changes show more clearly the deeper meaning of your parable. Depending on how many events your parable has, you might not use all three rows of the chart.

Events in your parable	Details of these events that could be exaggerated	How these exaggerations would better communicate the parable's deeper meaning

7

Christ in His Contexts

In this chapter you will read a parable from Isaiah that describes God's relationship with Israel through poignant imagery. Then you will examine the ways that Jesus used a wide range of Old Testament motifs, including Isaiah's imagery, to communicate more effectively with his Jewish audience. In examining this aspect of Jesus' ministry, you will learn about the roles that cultural and situational contexts play in providing his parables greater force and deeper meaning.

PART I: A Parable from Isaiah

Before Reading Consider…

- Why do you think the Bible often uses images of fruit and organic growth?
- What images or symbols carry special meaning in your culture?
- Do the examples that you cited from your own culture relate to any imagery or symbolism used in the Bible?

The Song of the Vineyard

(1) Let me sing for my beloved
  my love song concerning his vineyard:
My beloved had a vineyard
  on a very fertile hill.

(2) He dug it and cleared it of stones,
  and planted it with choice vines;
he built a watchtower in the midst of it,
  and hewed out a wine vat in it;

and he looked for it to yield grapes,
  but it yielded wild grapes.

(3) And now, O inhabitants of Jerusalem
  and men of Judah,
judge between me and my vineyard.

(4) What more was there to do for my vineyard,
  that I have not done in it?
When I looked for it to yield grapes,
  why did it yield wild grapes?

(5) And now I will tell you
  what I will do to my vineyard.
I will remove its hedge,
  and it shall be devoured;
I will break down its wall,
  and it shall be trampled down.

(6) I will make it a waste;
  it shall not be pruned or hoed,
  and briers and thorns shall grow up;
I will also command the clouds
  that they rain no rain upon it.

(7) For the vineyard of the LORD OF HOSTS
  is the house of Israel,
and the men of Judah
  are his pleasant planting;
and he looked for justice,
  but behold, bloodshed;
for righteousness, but behold, an outcry!
(Isaiah 5:1-7)

Notes/Questions

____

____

____

____

____

Theological Connection

1) This parable begins with very tender language. Much care has been lavished upon the vineyard, which represents Israel. What does this imagery communicate to Israel about its relationship to God?

____

____

____

2) Despite the cultivation of the vineyard, it produced "wild grapes," the same harvest as vines that do not receive such care. That is, even though God showed special love to Israel, it acted in the same unrighteousness way as the other nations that are without this privilege. In turn, what does the parable imply that God will do to Israel?

____

____

____

3) Commentators identify this parable as one of judgment.[1] John N. Oswalt connects it directly to the parable that Nathan told to David:

> In a way similar to Nathan's, when he used a story to get King David to condemn his own actions (2 Samuel 12:1-7), so Isaiah sets his hearers up to judge themselves: God has cared for them like a vineyard, yet the fruits of their lives are bitter and sour. Is not God more than justified if he decides to remove his protection from them?[2]

Review the parable principle for chapter 4, which examined Nathan's parable. Explain the intended effect of Isaiah's similar use of indirect communication.

____

____

____

1. David W. Pao and Eckhard J. Schnabel, "Luke" in G.K. Beale and D.A. Carson, ed., *Commentary on the New Testament Use of the Old Testament*, (Grand Rapids, MI: Baker Academic, 2007), 361 and Snodgrass, *Stories with Intent*, 40, 276.

2. John N. Oswalt, *The Book of Isaiah. The New International Commentary on the Old Testament Series* (Grand Rapids, MI: Eerdmans, 1998). 151-152.

PART II: Furthering Your Knowledge

Like Isaiah's parable, Jesus also used tender imagery to communicate God's love. Read the following passage about how Jesus employed the motifs of his culture to express his love for his people in the most intimate way. Read the left column if you want something more difficult or the right column for something easier. To ease your reading, the article has been divided into two parts.

As you read, underline parts you would like to ask questions about. Use the lines at the end of this reading to write down any questions you might have for your teacher.

Wells, Weddings, and Other Scenes with Samaritans (Part 1)

Difficult	Simplified
(1) A powerful technique in story telling is the use of culturally specific type-scenes. Robert Alter, a scholar of Hebrew literature, identifies several Old Testament type-scenes in *The Art of Biblical Narrative.* He describes this literary convention as "...dependent on the manipulation of a fixed constellation of predetermined motifs."[3] Essentially, it constitutes the particular *people, places,* and *procedures* in a scene that awaken certain expectations in the audience as to what will happen next.	(1) One tool that storytellers use is a type-scene. The scholar Robert Alter has shown that there are several examples of type-scenes in the Old Testament. A type-scene has three main aspects. It has certain people, places, and actions.[3] These parts are very familiar to the cultural audience and they make them think, "I know what will happen next."
(2) One such example that Alter examines is the betrothal type-scene. He points out that, generally, it follows five distinct procedures.[4]	(2) One Old Testament type-scene that Alter identifies is from stories about people preparing to be married. Five things happen.[4]

3. Robert Alter, *The Art of Biblical Narrative*, 2nd ed. (New York: Basic Books, 2011), 60.

4. Ibid., 61-69.

1) The man to be married, or his representative, travels to a foreign region.
2) There he meets a woman or multiple women at a well.
3) One of the parties collects water from the well.
4) The woman or women run to their home to announce the coming of the man into the foreign land.
5) The man at the well, or whom he represents, is betrothed to the woman or one woman among the group.

(3) Alter cites the betrothals of Isaac and Rebekah, Jacob and Rachel, and Moses and Zipporah as the clearest cases of this type-scene. The net result is that when an ancient Hebrew audience encountered an account of a man and woman at a well, they expected a marriage would follow.

(4) Alter is not a Christian and he addresses neither Jesus nor the New Testament. However, the betrothal type-scene supplies an important lens through which to better see Jesus' own encounter with a woman at a well. In John 4, Jesus has just left Judea and has stopped at a well in Samaria, a foreign region, en route to Galilee. He meets a woman there and asks for a drink. The request surprises her because he is a Jew, a people group who had "no dealings with Samaritans."[5]

1) The man (or his representative) goes to a foreign place.
2) There he meets a woman or many women at a well.
3) Someone gets water from the well.
4) The woman or women run home to tell that the man has come.
5) The man at the well (or the one whom he represents) and the woman (or one woman from the group) agree to marry.

(3) Alter gives examples from the lives of Isaac and Rebekah, Jacob and Rachel, and Moses and Zipporah. In turn, when a Hebrew audience came across a story about a man and woman at a well, they expected a marriage would follow.

(4) Alter is not a Christian and he does not talk about Jesus or the New Testament. However, this marriage type-scene is important in helping us understand the story of Jesus meeting a woman at a well. In John 4, Jesus has just left Judea and has stopped at a well in Samaria, a foreign region, on his way to Galilee. He meets a woman there and asks for a drink. The question surprises her because he is a Jew, a people group who did not talk with Samaritans.[5]

5. John 4:9.

(5) Then Jesus gives the type-scene a special significance, explaining that if she had known who he was, then she would have asked him for living water. This is the water that will quench our thirst eternally. From there, in line with both the expectations of the type-scene and the significance of his Messianic identity, Jesus raises the issue of marriage. He points out the woman's five previous husbands and the current man that she lives with. Lastly, in accordance with the prescribed procedures, the woman runs back to her village to announce Jesus' arrival. This produces an excited reception from her fellow residents.

(5) Then Jesus gives the scene a special meaning. He says that if she knew who he was, then she would ask him for living water. This is the water that will stop us from ever being thirsty again. Next, as with the other stories of that kind and because of who he is, Jesus talks about marriage. He says the woman has had five previous husbands and is now living with another man. Lastly, like all the type-scene stories, the woman runs back to her village to announce Jesus' arrival. The villagers are excited.

(6) Often, we find the scandal of this scene in the fact that Jesus was speaking to a person of female gender and Samaritan race, important details that certainly did make the disciples "marvel."[6] However, to an ancient Hebrew audience, and likely to the disciples upon reflection, the scandal goes much deeper than that. The last place that Jesus' Jewish contemporaries would have expected the Messiah to meet an adulterous, Samaritan woman was a well. The type-scene that Jesus has constructed would immediately produce the expectation of marriage between the two parties present. The scandal is not one of mere conversation, but of implied betrothal with a woman extremely offensive to his original audience.

(6) Often, we find it strange that Jesus was speaking to a woman who was also a Samaritan. Yes, those are important facts that made the disciples "marvel."[6] However, to ancient Hebrew readers, and probably for the disciples too when they thought about it, there was something even more strange. Why would the Messiah meet an adulterous, Samaritan woman at a well? This type-scene would make people think of marriage between the two parties present. This would have been shocking to the original audience.

6. John 4:27.

Notes/Questions

Think More About the Meaning

Complete the chart below by paraphrasing events from one of the Old Testament examples of the betrothal type-scene that the article cites (e.g., Isaac and Rebekah,[7] Jacob and Rachel,[8] or Moses and Zipporah[9]) and from John 4. Show how both specifically fulfill the required procedures of the scene. An example has been provided.

Type-Scene Procedure	Old Testament Example	John 4
The man to be married, or his representative, travels to a foreign region.		On his way from Judea to Galilee, Jesus comes to the Samaritan town of Sychar. He is tired from his journey so he sits beside a well.

7. Genesis 24.
8. Genesis 29.
9. Exodus 2.

There he meets a woman or multiple women at a well.		
One of the parties collects water from the well.		
The woman or women run to their home to announce the coming of the man into the foreign land.		
The man at the well, or whom he represents, is betrothed to the woman or one woman among the group.		There is no marriage in John 4, but how might this procedure relate to Jesus and the Samaritan woman?

Vocabulary Focus: Word Families[10]

The following words appear in the reading. Each word is part of a word family. Study the parts of the word families in the chart below. Look for spelling patterns for the noun, adjective and adverb forms of the words. Complete the chart and list the patterns in the spaces at the bottom of the chart. Some words do not have all four parts (--------).

Verb	Noun	Adjective	Adverb
construct	construction	constructive	constructively
describe	description	descriptive	
expect	expectation		expectantly
	identification; identity	identical	identically
manipulate		manipulative	--------------------
prescribe	prescription		--------------------
reflect		reflective	reflectively
reveal	revelation	revealing	
	significance	significant	significantly
surpass	---------------------		surpassingly
What spelling patterns can you identify in the nouns, adjectives, and adverbs? Write your responses on the chart.	*-ion*		

10. For this section, you can check your work with the Answer Key found in the back of this book.

Grammar Focus: Part of Speech[11]

Read each sentence and identify the part of speech of the missing word. Write in the appropriate form of the word in the blank. Use the word families' chart above to assist you. Discuss your answers with a partner.

Example

The type-scene that Jesus has constructed (construct) would produce the expectation (expect) of marriage between the two parties present.

1) The woman at the well waited ________________ (expect) for Jesus to answer her question.
2) The significance of Jesus' Messianic ____________ (identify) was not initially understood by the Samaritan woman.
3) She followed the ______________ (prescribe) procedures well.
4) His response to the question ________________ (surpass) her expectations.
5) The Samaritan woman's ___________ (describe) account of Jesus caused the townspeople to seek him out.
6) The Samaritans ______________ (reflect) on what the woman said about Jesus.
7) The _____________ (signify) of her testimony caused many to believe in Jesus.

Wells, Weddings, and Other Scenes with Samaritans (Part 2)

Difficult	Simplified
(1) Marriage is the most binding, demanding, and intimate relationship that can hold two humans together. A husband and a wife are even said to be of one flesh. As Paul writes of the matrimonial union, "This mystery is profound, and I am saying that it refers to Christ and the church."[12] And so marriage serves as a kind of human referent in understanding the relationship between Christ and his people.	(1) Marriage is the strongest and closest relationship that can hold two people together. A husband and a wife are even said to be of one flesh. As Paul writes of marriage, "This mystery is profound, and I am saying that it refers to Christ and the church."[12] And so marriage serves as a kind of human way of understanding the relationship between Christ and his people.

11. For this section, you can check your work with the Answer Key found in the back of this book.
12. Ephesians 5:32.

(2) As such, Jesus really does become the bridegroom of the Samaritan woman. To the same degree that his living water surpasses the stagnant water of the well, so Christ's devotion to his bride surpasses that of the six men she has previously known. And of course, all of the church is his bride. As a great multitude sings in the book of Revelation:

> Let us rejoice and exult
> and give him the glory,
> for the marriage of the Lamb has come,
> and his Bride has made herself ready;
> it was granted to clothe herself with fine linen, bright and pure.[13]

The church is his bride because this identity has been "granted" to us. As has often and rightly been said, Christ loved us not because we were lovely, but to make us lovely. And through his person and work, he has made us and is making us lovely indeed, preparing us for the marriage celebration that is to come.

(3) With these truths in mind, it is a good exercise to transpose the Samaritan well scene onto the betrothal type-scenes of our own cultures. For instance, in the West, one such scene places a woman on a balcony looking down upon a man standing on the ground below. *Romeo and Juliet* perhaps gives us the most famous example, with Romeo declaring, "But, soft! What light through yonder window breaks? It is the east, and Juliet is the sun."[14]

(2) Therefore, in a sense, Jesus really does become the bridegroom of the Samaritan woman. Just as his living water is greater than the unmoving water of the well, so Christ's love for his bride is more than the love of the six men she has known before. And of course, all of the church is his bride. As a great crowd sings in the book of Revelation:

> Let us rejoice and exult
> and give him the glory,
> for the marriage of the Lamb has come,
> and his Bride has made herself ready;
> it was granted to clothe herself with fine linen, bright and pure.[13]

The church is his bride because this identity has been "granted" to us. As has often and rightly been said, Christ loved us not because we were lovely, but to make us lovely. And through his person and work, he has made us and is making us lovely indeed, preparing us for the future marriage celebration.

(3) Remembering these truths, it is a good exercise to change the Samaritan well scene into the betrothal type-scenes of our own cultures. For instance, in the West, one such scene places a woman on a balcony looking down upon a man standing on the ground below. *Romeo and Juliet* perhaps gives us the most famous example, with Romeo declaring, "But, soft! What light through yonder window breaks? It is the east, and Juliet is the sun."[14]

13. Revelation 19:7-8.
14. Act 2, Scene 2.

(4) Even current movies use this scene, although they change it to fit modern architecture. Such films show a suitor standing on the sidewalk below the bedroom window of his beloved. The boy throws stones at her window and hopes that she will peak out from her second-story perch.

(5) Similarly, in Southeast Asian culture, a traditional betrothal type-scene brings together a man and a woman who meet for the first time working the fields of a rice paddy. They begin to sing in poetry to each other and immediately the audience anticipates their future marriage. In turn, depending on one's respective culture, it is helpful to picture Jesus coming upon the Samaritan woman who stands on a balcony high above him or plodding through paddies toward her with a plow in-hand. Of course, the purpose is not to change the text. Christ has specifically revealed himself in the scene described in John 4 and that alone is special revelation.

(6) However, Christ incarnated himself amidst the culture of first-century Palestine and ministered accordingly. In turn, as we communicate Christ both to ourselves and to others, we should appeal to our own cultural equivalents. Personally, when I imagine the encounter with Jesus calling up to the woman in the balcony, it produces a reaction that simply acknowledging the Hebrew type-scene cannot. It makes me feel firsthand the severe scandal of the scene. And with that, the supreme hope.

(4) Even today movies use this scene, although they change it to fit modern architecture. Such films show a young man standing on the sidewalk below the bedroom window of his beloved. The boy throws stones at her window and hopes that she will look out from her second-story perch.

(5) Similarly, in Southeast Asian culture, a traditional betrothal type-scene brings together a man and a woman who meet for the first time working the fields of a rice paddy. They begin to sing in poetry to each other and immediately the audience knows there will be a future marriage. In turn, depending on our culture, it is helpful to picture Jesus coming upon the Samaritan woman who stands on a balcony high above him or plodding through paddies toward her with a plow in-hand. Of course, the purpose is not to change the text. Christ has revealed himself clearly in the scene described in John 4 and that alone is special revelation.

(6) However, Christ became man in the culture of first-century Palestine and ministered in that culture. In turn, as we talk about Christ both to ourselves and to others, we should look at our own culture. Personally, when I imagine the meeting, with Jesus calling up to the woman in the balcony, it gives me a feeling that doesn't come from the Hebrew type-scene. It makes me feel firsthand the severe scandal of the scene. And with that, the high hope.

(7) Unlike the perfect revelation of the well scene, however, a balcony has no place for a reference to "living water." With that said, the intricacy through which Christ has revealed himself in Scripture should amaze us.	(7) Unlike the perfect revelation of the well scene, however, a balcony has no place for talking about "living water." However, the details through which Christ has revealed himself in Scripture should amaze us.

Think More About the Meaning

1) Can you identify a betrothal type-scene in your culture? If so, what is it and how does it affect you when you transpose the scene from John 4 onto it?

____

____

____

____

2) Throughout Scripture, the relation of Christ to his church is communicated through a number of images. For example, Christ is our bridegroom, our shepherd, and our physician. Choose one of these images and explain what it communicates to you about Christ.

____

____

____

____

3) The book of Luke ends with the following description of the disciples' response to Christ after the resurrection, "And they worshiped him and returned to Jerusalem with great joy, and were continually in the temple blessing God."[15] Commenting on this passage, Michael Wilcock writes:

> So it is in the temple that Luke not only begins but also ends his gospel (24:53); the important thing now, however, is not the old building, which is doomed to destruction, but the community of Jesus's people gathered there. Henceforth it is they who "are God's temple", and among them God is to be met with.[16]

15. Luke 24:52-53.
16. Wilcock, *The Savior of the World*, 215.

From the silencing of Zechariah to the praise of the disciples, Luke's Gospel ends in the same place it began. The people of God have returned to the temple but everything has changed. And the temple itself has come to be understood in a different way. That is, God's people are the temple in which he will dwell. Similarly, how does Jesus change the understanding of the well? How does the expectation of marriage it produces come to signify the truth of a closer relationship with God?

____

____

____

____

____

____

____

____

Vocabulary Strategy: Understanding Word Parts

There are three word-parts of English words. They are the prefix, the root and the suffix. The root of the word carries the meaning of the word. The prefix changes the meaning of the word and the suffix indicates the part of speech. Prefixes come before the root word and suffixes come after the root word. Prefixes and suffixes are called affixes.

<u>*Example*</u>

Word	Prefix	Root	Suffix	Part of Speech	Meaning
unforgivable	un	forgive	able	adjective	so bad that it cannot be forgiven

Identifying Roots[17]

A lot of words in English are based upon roots that have a meaning. For example the word *theology* contains the roots *theo* (related to God) and *logy* (a subject of study). Identifying the meaning of common word roots can help in understanding the meaning of unfamiliar words.

Underline the root in the following words.

Example

unrighteous

1) predetermined
2) expectations
3) significance
4) procedures
5) revelation
6) betrothal
7) matrimonial
8) unhappiness
9) unprepared
10) similarly
11) irrespective
12) incarnation
13) culturally
14) acknowledgement

➡ Understanding Affixes

As stated previously, English words change their forms when adding a prefix (a word part added to the beginning of a word) and a suffix (adding a word part to the end of a word). Prefixes and suffixes are called affixes.

Some affixes change a word's part of speech.

verb + tion = noun — Example: describe (verb) = description

verb + ive = adjective — Example: describe (verb) = descriptive

verb + ly = adverb — Example: describe (verb) = descriptively

17. For this section, you can check your work with the Answer Key found in the back of this book.

Identifying Prefixes[18]

Underline the prefix in each word. Write a sentence for each word.

Example

nonprofit — She works for a nonprofit organization.

1) unrighteous ______________________

2) unbelievable ______________________

3) outrun ______________________

4) co-sponsor ______________________

5) multinational ______________________

6) unilateral ______________________

7) bicultural ______________________

8) unbelievable ______________________

9) undercurrent ______________________

10) unholy ______________________

18. For this section, you can check your work with the Answer Key found in the back of this book.

Identifying Suffixes[19]

Underline the suffix in each word. Identify the part of speech (noun, verb, adjective, adverb)

Word	Part of Speech	Sentence
Example		
nonverb<u>al</u>	adjective	Hand gestures are an important part of nonverbal communication.
1) multicultural	________	________________
2) holiness	________	________________
3) spirituality	________	________________
4) co-sponsorship	________	________________
5) communicatively	________	________________
6) betrothal	________	________________
7) Protestantism	________	________________
8) orthodoxy	________	________________
9) righteousness	________	________________
10) justly	________	________________

19. For this section, you can check your work with the Answer Key found in the back of this book.

Putting It All Together[20]

Identify the word parts in each word and complete the chart below.

Word	Prefix	Root	Suffix	Part of Speech	Meaning
Example **unrighteous**	**un**	**right**	**eous**	**adjective**	**not doing right**
undernourished					
predestination					
unpardonable					
unfortunately					
regeneration					

PART III: A Parable of Jesus

Before Reading Consider…

In chapter 4, we examined a parable from the prophet Nathan. At the beginning of this chapter, we investigated one from Isaiah. These parables, as well as other examples of this genre in the Old Testament, have much hermeneutical significance when interpreting those of Jesus. As Klyne Snodgrass writes:

> The primary influence on Jesus' use of parables is the OT. The form of Jesus' parables, the parabolic way of thinking, the images used, and the use of parables in wisdom literature and especially as prophetic instruments all point in that direction.[21]

In particular, the following parable from Jesus employs the same "image used" in Isaiah's parable. That is, Jesus revisits the image of the vineyard and its reference to Israel.

20. For this section, you can check your work with the Answer Key found in the back of this book.

21. Snodgrass, *Stories with Intent*, 38.

Why do you think Jesus chose to employ this image with his Jewish audience?

How does Jesus' use of vineyard imagery relate to his use of the betrothal type-scene in John 4?

Kevin Vanhoozer urges us to recognize that interpreting Scripture is more than just extracting information. We must also learn to experience the Bible in ways that are appropriate to each of its literary genres. "It involves acquiring the cognitive skills and sensibilities, and hence *the ability to see, feel, and taste the world as disclosed in the diverse biblical texts.*"[22]

Reflecting on the importance of experiencing a text, complete the following chart.

Culturally meaningful image	**Feelings this image produced in Hebrew audience**	**Ways of reading that can help you experience similar feelings**
A man and woman at a well		
A vineyard		

22. Vanhoozer, *The Drama of Doctrine*, 285.

Situational Context

Just before Jesus tells the following parable, his opponents question his authority to teach and preach. Luke writes:

> One day, as Jesus was teaching the people in the temple and preaching the gospel, the chief priests and the scribes with the elders came up and said to him, "Tell us by what authority you do these things, or who it is that gave you this authority." He answered them, "I also will ask you a question. Now tell me, was the baptism of John from heaven or from man?" And they discussed it with one another, saying, "If we say, 'From heaven,' he will say, 'Why did you not believe him?' But if we say, 'From man,' all the people will stone us to death, for they are convinced that John was a prophet." So they answered that they did not know where it came from. And Jesus said to them, "Neither will I tell you by what authority I do these things." (Luke 20:1-8)

Jesus declines to directly answer this question about his authority, but he then goes on to respond though a parable.[23] This parable not only establishes his own authority, but also rejects the authority of his opponents.

Reflect on the question, "Who is it that gave you this authority?" Consider how the chief priests, scribes, and elders would have answered their own question. Then complete the chart below.

Question	**Answer**
What do you think their answer to this question would have been?	
Why do you think they saw Jesus as a threat to their authority?	

23. Green, *The Gospel of Luke*, 703.

What do you think they were willing to do to protect their authority?	

The Parable of the Wicked Tenants

And he began to tell the people this parable: "A man planted a vineyard and let it out to tenants and went into another country for a long while. When the time came, he sent a servant to the tenants, so that they would give him some of the fruit of the vineyard. But the tenants beat him and sent him away empty-handed. And he sent another servant. But they also beat and treated him shamefully, and sent him away empty-handed. And he sent yet a third. This one also they wounded and cast out. Then the owner of the vineyard said, 'What shall I do? I will send my beloved son; perhaps they will respect him.' But when the tenants saw him, they said to themselves, 'This is the heir. Let us kill him, so that the inheritance may be ours.' And they threw him out of the vineyard and killed him. What then will the owner of the vineyard do to them? He will come and destroy those tenants and give the vineyard to others." When they heard this, they said, "Surely not!" But he looked directly at them and said, "What then is this that is written:

> "'The stone that the builders rejected
> has become the cornerstone'?

Everyone who falls on that stone will be broken to pieces, and when it falls on anyone, it will crush him."

The scribes and the chief priests sought to lay hands on him at that very hour, for they perceived that he had told this parable against them, but they feared the people.

(Luke 20:9-19)

Important Cultural Information

- Tenant arrangements, like the one described in the parable, were regular practices. Additionally, disputes between landowners and their tenants were not uncommon.[24]

24. Snodgrass, *Stories with Intent*, 284.

Examining the Parable

David W. Pao and Eckhard J. Schnabel provide a helpful two-fold focus for interpreting this parable. They write, "The parable draws its meaning from two contexts: the designation of Jesus as God's 'beloved son' and the OT background of Isaiah 5:1–7."[25] We will investigate both of these contexts below.

Old Testament Background of Isaiah 5:1-7

1) For Jesus' audience, the image of the vineyard would have immediately brought to mind God's relationship to his people as illustrated in Isaiah's parable. However, in contrast to Isaiah 5:1-7, it is not the vineyard that receives judgment but the tenants who are tending the vineyard.[26] In turn, who do you think Jesus is condemning in this parable, Israel or its leaders? Why?

____

____

____

____

____

2) After Jesus tells the parable, Luke informs us that the leaders of Israel recognize that the parable is meant to condemn them. They know that the wicked tenants represent them and their leadership. Understanding that the owner of the vineyard represents God, what does the parable communicate about these leaders and their relationship to God?

____

____

____

____

____

---

25. Green, *The Gospel of Luke*, 705.

26. Pao and Schnabel, "Luke" in *Commentary on the Old Testament's Use of the Old Testament*, 362.

3) Reflect on the question of authority that framed the context for this parable. What is Jesus' intended message concerning the authority of the chief priests, scribes, and elders?

____

____

____

____

Jesus as God's "Beloved Son"

1) The last person the landowner sends to the wicked tenants is his "beloved son." By this description, Jesus asserts his identity as the Son of God. As Klyne Snodgrass comments on this title and the treatment this beloved son receives, "...we must say that this is the most revealing parable about Jesus' own sense of his role in God's purposes and was a precipitating factor leading to his arrest."[27]

   What is Jesus revealing about the source of his authority by his use of "beloved son?"

____

____

____

____

2) When the tenants find out that the landowner's son is coming, they say to themselves, "This is the heir. Let us kill him, so that the inheritance may be ours." How does this statement relate to the actions Israel's leaders would carry out to protect their authority against Jesus?

____

____

____

____

27. Snodgrass, *Stories with Intent*, 298.

3) Jesus concludes the parable with a pronouncement of judgment using the imagery of a stone, quoting Psalm 118:22 and alluding to Isaiah 8:14-15 and Daniel 2:34 and 2:44-45.[28] To Jesus' Jewish audience, the stone functioned as an image for the Messiah.[29]

   Reflect on Jesus' stone imagery. What are the implications of this imagery for his identity? What is he expressing about the rejection he will endure, the glory he will receive, and the judgment he will bring?

   ____

   ____

   ____

   ____

   ____

4) In John 5:22-23, Jesus says, "The Father judges no one, but has given all judgment to the Son, that all may honor the Son, just as they honor the Father. Whoever does not honor the Son does not honor the Father who sent him." Review the interpretive aspect of *Testimony to Christ* from chapter 5. Explain how this passage from John testifies to the message of the parable of the wicked tenants.

   ____

   ____

   ____

Love and Sending

(1) This parable places much emphasis on the act of sending. After sending his servants to the wicked tenants, the landowner sent his own "beloved son." Of course, God the Father has also sent his only begotten Son into our wicked world. As a result, the Son of God endured shameful treatment similar to what was experienced by the son in the parable. In light of this suffering, why would God the Father choose to send his Son to us?

28. Pao and Schnabel, "Luke" in *Commentary on the Old Testament's Use of the Old Testament*, 362-363.
29. Ibid., 364-365.

(2) John's Gospel reveals much about the relationships between the divine persons within the Trinity. In particular, it demonstrates the intimate connection between Trinitarian love and Trinitarian sending. Even more, it shows us how the church is brought into these actions. Christ tells his disciples, "As the Father has loved me, so have I loved you."[30] That is, the Father's love for the Son propels Christ's love for us. Similarly, the resurrected Christ commissions his disciples with the words, "As the Father has sent me, even so I am sending you."[31] Again we find the progression from the Father to the Son to the church. The Father sends Christ and Christ sends us. Then, in conclusion of this commission, Christ shows us who empowers the church to fulfill his mission to the world. John writes, "And when he had said this, he breathed on them and said to them, 'Receive the Holy Spirit.'"[32] And so we see that each person in the Trinity plays a distinct and essential role in this sending love and loving sending.

(3) Michael Reeves summarizes well the connection between the eternal love of the Trinity and the mission it motivates. He writes:

> So the Father sent the Son because of how he so loved him (and wanted *that* love to be shared and enjoyed), and the Son went because he so loved his Father (and wanted *that* love to be shared and enjoyed). The mission comes from the overflow of love, from the uncontainable enjoyment of the fellowship.
>
> So it is with the Father and the Son; so it is with us. The Spirit catches us up to share their pleasure, and it is that delight in them that fuels us to *want* to make them known.[33]

Reflecting on these three paragraphs, use their main ideas to complete the five sentences in the diagram on the following page. Discuss your reflections with your classmates.

30. John 15:9.

31. John 20:21.

32. John 20:22.

33. Michael Reeves, *Delighting in the Trinity: An Introduction to the Christian Faith* (Downers Grove, IL: InterVarsity, 2012), 106.

The Father …

The Son …

The Spirit …

The Church …

The World …

PART IV: Writing Your Own Parable

> **Parable Principle 7**
> Jesus told parables in particular cultural and situational contexts. Jesus' audience was composed of people living in the culture of first-century Palestine and his parables used elements that were accessible, relevant, and meaningful to that culture. Additionally, his parables were often a response to the words and actions that someone else had directed at him. In turn, when we interpret Jesus' parables, we must seek to understand the culture they were told within and the situation that prompted them.

In this chapter we have seen how Jesus used images that were meaningful to his Jewish audience to communicate his person and work with added force and depth. His actions at the well showed us that he is our true bridegroom. Similarly, the vineyard setting of the above parable alerted his audience that he was addressing God's relationship with Israel.

What implications does the importance of cultural and situational context have for your own Bible study?

____

____

____

____

Matthew, Mark, and Luke all place their version of the parable of the wicked tenants in between the same events. It follows the questioning of Jesus' authority by Israel's leaders and precedes their asking whether taxes should be paid to Caesar.[34] Both events bring issues of authority to the forefront, as the authority of Jesus, God, and Caesar is addressed. How does this situational context help us to properly interpret the parable? What do these three gospel writers want us to focus on?

____

____

____

34. Snodgrass, *Stories with Intent,* 282. The other versions of this parable are found in Matthew 21:33-46 and Mark 12:1-12. However, Matthew does place a series of three parables between these two events in which Jesus' authority was challenged. The parable of the tenants is the second of the three.

Now think about the parable you are writing. Considering the cultural and situational context you will tell your parable within, complete the following chart.

What is the culture of your parable's audience?	
What culturally meaningful images or symbols could you use in your parable?	
What do these images or symbols represent?	
What words, actions, or circumstances might prompt your parable?	

8

Putting It All Together

> This was to fulfill what was spoken by the prophet:
> "I will open my mouth in parables;
> I will utter what has been hidden since the foundation of the world."
> Matthew 13:35

Congratulations. Because of your hard work, you have completed the seven chapters in this text. You have read and studied different parables from around the world and from the gospel of Luke. You have reflected on and discussed different aspects of theology and have identified different structural and lexical challenges contained in theological writing.

You have been challenged to read more efficiently by implementing reading and vocabulary strategies. You have had opportunities to discuss and interact with your classmates through oral exercises. You have engaged with different principles that characterize parables. You have also had the opportunity to integrate these principles by writing your own parable.

In this chapter you will have the opportunity to put these principles into use by identifying them in one of the following parables. You will also have space to write out your parable and identify the various principles in your parable. Once you have completed this exercise you may want to present your parable to your class, small group, partner or teacher.

Here is a procedure that integrates the four skills in your presentation: First, read your parable aloud to the class. Encourage them to listen carefully. After reading the parable, give them a printed copy to read silently. Lead them through a series of questions about your parable. What principles can they identify? What is its teaching? Are there cultural lessons in the parable? Finally, put all of your parables into one notebook so that others can read them. Focus on other parables of Jesus not found in this text and go through a similar procedure as the one outlined above.

The authors hope this final chapter will help you put what you have learned in the preceding chapters into practice. The process of listening, reading, writing, and talking about parables and the theological connections will help you become better readers of theological publications written in English.

Parable Principles

Parable Principle 1

Jesus' parables are concise, to the point, and have a very important purpose. These were not just stories to entertain his audience. He told them to change the beliefs, attitudes, and behaviors of his listeners.

Parable Principle 2

Parables contain two levels of meaning. There is the surface meaning of the actual story told and the deeper meaning to which the story points. So then, in Jesus' parables, what is the deeper level of meaning that each surface story points to? The deeper meaning is the revelation of the kingdom of God.

Parable Principle 3

The characters of parables are usually human. Some of Jesus' parables focus on things like birds, seeds, and weeds. However, in contrast to a fable, these things are not given human characteristics.

Parable Principle 4

Parables are a form of indirect communication. Instead of directly confronting a belief, attitude, or behavior present in their audience, parables use much more subtle means. They are stories that attract and hold the interest of their hearers. These hearers are so absorbed in the story that they do not realize they have been confronted until the story is over. Having listened attentively, the audience, to their surprise, has seen an issue from a new perspective.

Parable Principle 5

Parables frequently have a purpose of concealing, as well as revealing. An audience often needs additional explanation to grasp the intended meaning of the parable. In such cases, the story alone is not enough for adequate understanding.

Parable Principle 6

Parables contain events common in the normal life of their audience. However, in order to call attention to their deeper meanings, parables usually communicate these events in exaggerated ways. These exaggerated elements will often seem improbable but, in Jesus' parables, they forcefully direct his audience to the truths of his kingdom.

Parable Principle 7

Jesus told parables in particular cultural and situational contexts. Jesus' audience was composed of people living in the culture of first-century Palestine and his parables used elements that were accessible, relevant, and meaningful to that culture. Additionally, his parables were often a response to the words and actions that someone else had directed at him. In turn, when we interpret Jesus' parables, we must seek to understand the culture they were told within and the situation that prompted them.

Two Parables from Luke

Choose one of the two parables below. Identify the principles that appear in the parable. Discuss your findings with a partner.

The Parable of the Rich Fool

Someone in the crowd said to him, "Teacher, tell my brother to divide the inheritance with me." But he said to him, "Man, who made me a judge or arbitrator over you?" And he said to them, "Take care, and be on your guard against all covetousness, for one's life does not consist in the abundance of his possessions." And he told them a parable, saying, "The land of a rich man produced plentifully, and he thought to himself, 'What shall I do, for I have nowhere to store my crops?' And he said, 'I will do this: I will tear down my barns and build larger ones, and there I will store all my grain and my goods. And I will say to my soul, "Soul, you have ample goods laid up for many years; relax, eat, drink, be merry."' But God said to him, 'Fool! This night your soul is required of you, and the things you have prepared, whose will they be?' So is the one who lays up treasure for himself and is not rich toward God."

(Luke 12:13-21)

____

____

____

____

____

____

The Parable of the Pharisee and the Tax Collector

He also told this parable to some who trusted in themselves that they were righteous, and treated others with contempt: "Two men went up into the temple to pray, one a Pharisee and the other a tax collector. The Pharisee, standing by himself, prayed thus: 'God, I thank you that I am not like other men, extortioners, unjust, adulterers, or even like this tax collector. I fast twice a week; I give tithes of all that I get.' But the tax collector, standing far off, would not even lift up his eyes to heaven, but beat his breast, saying, 'God, be merciful to me, a sinner!' I tell you, this man went down to his house justified, rather than the other. For everyone who exalts himself will be humbled, but the one who humbles himself will be exalted."

(Luke 18:9-14)

Putting It All Together

Write your parable in the space below. Identify the parable principles integrated into your parable. Share your parable with the class.

Title:
Author:

Answer Key

This section contains answers for selected exercises from chapters 1 through 7. For some items where there is more than one acceptable response to a question, a suggested response might be included. For other items with more than one correct response, there is simply the statement of "Answers may vary."

CHAPTER 1

➲ *Reading Strategy: Put These In Order (p. 5)*

1) Use numbers 1-8

__6__ A holy man came along.

__2__ The farmer saw the tiger's tail on the path.

__8__ The holy man said he could not kill the tiger.

__4__ The farmer quickly took hold of the tail and held on.

__1__ An Indonesian farmer was on his way home.

__7__ The farmer begged him to kill the tiger with his scythe.

__3__ The farmer put down his scythe.

__5__ The tiger struggled to get loose.

2) Use numbers 9-15

__13__ The farmer picked up his scythe and started to leave.

__11__ The holy man thought there was no harm in holding the tiger's tail.

__9__ The farmer was wet with sweat.

__12__ The holy man was holding on to the tiger's tail.

__14__ The farmer explained that he had been converted to the holy man's religion.

__10__ The farmer wanted the holy man to hold on to the tiger's tail so that he could kill the beast.

__15__ The holy man would have to hold on to the tiger's tail until someone else came along to help.

Vocabulary Focus (p. 6)

1) k. roar
2) i. religious act
3) f. religion
4) a. carefully
5) l. fierce
6) g. thought
7) b. stopped
8) d. change
9) c. angry

Vocabulary Focus (p. 9)

1) Two words mean "to make holy." The words are *consecration* and *sanctification.*
2) One word means to *devote* ourselves to the service or worship of God.
3) The second word means to make the person *pure.*
4) The two words are important for people and for all *creation.*
5) How can the world be *cleansed* of its sin?
6) For some *infectious* illnesses we have to go away from other people.
7) With the help of the Holy Spirit, we work to *sanctify* our families and our communities.
8) As things are *sanctified* they will be consecrated because they will stand out from others like them.

CHAPTER 2

Vocabulary Focus (p. 22)

1) **token** (noun) Something that serves as a symbol.
2) **discerned** (verb) To make sense of.
3) **plot** (noun) A fairly small piece of ground.
4) **overheard** (verb) To hear without the speaker's knowledge.
5) **dismissed** (verb) To send away.
6) **perplexed** (verb) To cause a person to feel confused.
7) **breed (bred)** (verb) To produce offspring, children, or in this case livestock.

8) **steward** (noun) A person who is appointed by a master to take care of the master's affairs.

9) **simply** (adverb) In a plain manner.

10) **better** (adjective) Of superior quality.

Grammar Focus (p. 28)

1) The *Westminster Shorter Catechism* states that, "Man's chief end is to glorify God and to enjoy him forever."	infinitive
2) We enjoy glorifying him in our daily work.	gerund
3) We are called to glorify him in the present age.	infinitive
4) It means the next age has begun breaking into our current age.	gerund
5) He finished reading the *Westminster Shorter Catechism* at midnight.	gerund
6) He prepared to go to the church and to preach his sermon.	infinitive

Grammar Focus (p. 33)

Organizational Marker 1	Organizational Marker 2	Organizational Marker 3
Firstly	Secondly	Thirdly
Realm of God's saving grace	Realm of righteousness and justice	Realm of God's blessing and joy
Bible reference: Answers may vary	Bible reference: Answers may vary	Bible reference: Answers may vary

CHAPTER 3

Grammar Focus (p. 38)

Organizational Marker 1	Organizational Marker 2	Organizational Marker 3
First	Then	Finally
Sentence: First the eldest son spoke.	Sentence: Then the second son spoke.	Sentence: Finally it was the third son's turn to speak.

1) Adverb: suddenly — Sentence: Suddenly he fell in as I watched.
2) Adverb: easily — Sentence: …so I could easily have helped myself to some of them
3) Adverb: immediately — Sentence: I recognized him immediately.
4) Adverb: angrily — Sentence: He shouted at me angrily.
5) Adverb: really — Sentence: That is a really noble deed.

Vocabulary Focus (p. 39)

1) e. pleasing to the eye; lovely
2) c. of great value
3) g. to be sorry about something
4) f. steep cliff; overhanging rock
5) a. having high moral qualities or greatness
6) h. valuable ring, necklace or gem
7) d. one who buys and sells things
8) b. unsafe; likely to cause injury

Vocabulary Focus (p. 50)

	Word	Definition	Sentence
1)	squandered	to waste	The child squandered his allowance on candy.
2)	reckless	careless, without concern	His behavior was reckless.
3)	hired	paid to do a service	I hired John to paint the house.

4) embraced	to be included	He was embraced as part of the family.
5) celebrate	to observe	Every year we celebrate Christmas.
6) disobeyed	refuse to listen	The soldier disobeyed direct orders.
7) devoured	totally destroyed	The fire devoured the building.

CHAPTER 4

Reading Strategy (p. 60)

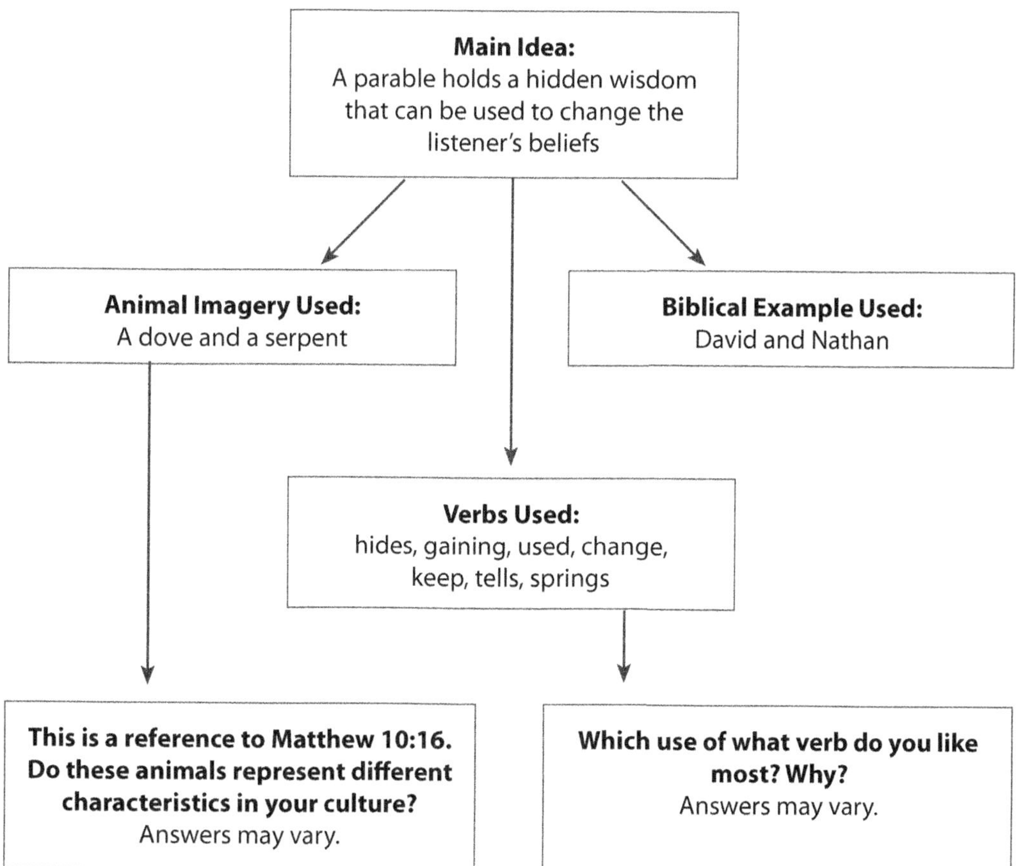

Word Selection (p. 64)

1) fulfillment
2) interpretive
3) typology
4) priest, threefold
5) prophet
6) identity

➲ *Grammar Focus: Indirect Speech (p. 69)*

Simon said to give him that power also, so that anyone on whom he laid his hands

1 2 3 2 5 2

might receive the Holy Spirit.

4

Peter told Simon that he had neither part nor lot in that matter, for his heart was not

1 2 4 3 2 4

right before God.

CHAPTER 5

➲ *Vocabulary Focus: Word Forms (p. 85)*

1) purposes, verb
2) magnificent, adjective
3) imposed, verb
4) continually, adverb
5) created, verb
6) fulfillment, noun
7) transformed, verb
8) righteousness, noun

➲ *Poetic Form (p. 90) – possible answers*

First Comparison

Sentence 1: The unrighteous judge reluctantly gives justice to the widow.

Sentence 2: God gives justice speedily to his elect.

Combine these with *while:* The unrighteous judge reluctantly gives justice to the widow, while God gives justice speedily to his elect.

Second Comparison

Sentence 1: The unrighteous judge grows weary of widow's plea for justice.

Sentence 2: God does not grow weary of those who cry to him day and night.

Combine these sentences with *although:* Although the unrighteous judge grows weary of the widow's plea for justice, God does not grow weary of those who cry to him day and night.

➲ *Testimony to Jesus Christ (p. 94) – possible answers*

Paragraph 1

Parables can hold an eschatological significance that tells us what will happen when Christ returns and the kingdom of God fully arrives on earth.

Paragraph 2

This parable gives us assurance that God's justice is certain, so we should have faith in him even in the midst of hardship.

Paragraph 3

The parable reminds us of the "already but not yet" dynamic of the Kingdom: even though we have severe suffering now, soon Christ will vindicate His followers in full.

CHAPTER 6

➲ *Vocabulary Focus (p. 104) – definitions may vary*

1) announces (verb): to make something known
2) rushed upon (phrasal verb): filled, empowered, inhabited
3) offspring (noun): children, descendants
4) fulfillment (noun): the state of being fulfilled; the keeping or completion of a promise
5) lineage (noun): the direct line of descent; a person's ancestors and descendants
6) recounts (verb): tells the story of
7) compromise (verb): discredit, damage, hinder
   divine (adjective): of God, supernatural

➲ *Vocabulary Strategy: Identifying Noun Suffixes in Context (p. 106) (words from readings on p. 101-103 and p. 108-109)*

-ion/-tion/-ation	-ship	-ment	-ness	Other suffix ending
completion	kingship	fulfillment	childlessness	adulthood
proclamation	sonship	judgment		baptism
expectation				kingdom
temptation(s)				Holiness *
inauguration *				
crucifixion *				
rejection *				
declaration *				
introduction *				
resurrection *				

***=words from the reading on p. 108-109)**

Words in order of appearance in readings:
p. 101

1) kingship (ship)
2) fulfillment (ment)
3) completion (ion)

p. 102

1) childlessness (ness)
2) adulthood (other)
3) judgment (ment)
4) baptism (other)
5) proclamation (ation)
6) fulfillment (ment)
7) expectation (ation)
8) kingdom (other)

p. 103

1) fulfillment (ment)
2) kingship (ship)
3) baptism (other)
4) temptations (ation)
5) sonship (ship)
6) temptations (ation)
7) sonship (ship)

p. 108

1) inauguaration (ation)
2) kingship (ship)
3) expectations (ation)
4) crucifixion (ion)
5) sonship (ship)
6) rejection (ion)
7) rejection (ion)
8) sonship (ship)
9) declaration (ation)

p. 109

1) introduction (tion)
2) resurrection (ion)
3) kingship (ship)
4) sonship (ship)
5) holiness (ness)
6) resurrection (ion)
7) sonship (ship)
8) resurrection (tion)
9) declaration (tion)

➲ *Vocabulary Focus (p. 112) – definitions may vary*

1) pronounce (verb): speak, proclaim
2) mocked (verb): ridiculed, made fun of

3) messianic (adjective): pertaining to the Messiah
4) divine (adjective): pertaining to God, supernatural
5) inauguration (noun): beginning, commencement
6) rejection (noun): refusal to receive, accept or consider someone or something
7) anointed (verb): set apart and empowered for ministry
8) declaration (noun): clear announcement

Grammar Focus: Noun Clauses (p. 114)

1) The gospel according to Luke announces that Jesus is the long awaited king in the line of David.
2) Many of the events surrounding the life of Jesus, which Luke recounts, parallel events that establish David's kingship.
3) Wright points out how Luke's opening chapters correspond with many happenings in the book of 1 Samuel.
4) The same Spirit that rushed upon David descends upon Jesus in the form of a dove.
5) I will raise up your offspring after you, who shall come from your body, and I will establish his kingdom.
6) The last link in the messianic family line tells us that Jesus is the Son of God.
7) Are you the one who is to come, or shall we look for another?
8) We are the ones who deserved that rejection of sonship.

Fluency Practice: Put the Sentences of the Dialogue in Order (p. 116)

7 Now, who's next?

18 Just a minute. He already has ten minas!

10 Lord, I have been careful with your money. Here is your one mina. I kept it safely in a handkerchief. Do you want to know why?

3 Good. Now let me see the person over there. What happened to your money?

19 I tell you that to everyone who has, more will be given, but from the one who has not, even what he has will be taken away.

17 You did. Now listen everyone. Take the mina from this last man, and give it to the one who has the ten minas.

1 Everyone please work hard until I come back.

9 I'm pleased with you. You can lead five cities. Third person, please.

4 Lord, your one mina has made ten minas more.

11 Yes. Why did you do that?

13 Sorry but you have not done a good thing. If you knew that I was a severe man, taking what I did not deposit and reaping what I did not sow, then why then did you not put my money in the bank?

5 That's great. You are a good servant! Because you have worked hard with only a little money I'll make you the leader of ten cities.

12 I was afraid of you, because you are a severe man. You take what you did not deposit, and reap what you did not sow.

15 Because then on my return I could have collected it with interest.

8 It's me. Look, your one mina has made five minas.

14 Why would I put it in the bank?

6 Thank you. Off I go to lead ten cities.

2 Now I'm back. Everyone who had money please come here.

16 Oh dear. I did the wrong thing.

CHAPTER 7

Vocabulary Focus: Word Families (p. 135)

Verb	Noun	Adjective	Adverb
What spelling patterns can you identify in the nouns, adjectives, and adverbs?	-ion, -tion, -ation, -ication, -ance	-ive,- tive, -ant, -tant, -cal, -ing	-ly

Grammar Focus: Part of Speech (p. 136)

1) expectantly (adverb)
2) identity (noun)
3) prescription (noun)
4) surpassed, surpasses (verb)
5) descriptive (adjective)
6) reflected, reflect (verb)
7) significance (noun)

Identifying Roots (p. 141)

1) predetermined
2) expectations
3) significance
4) procedures
5) revelation
6) betrothal
7) matrimonial
8) unhappiness
9) unprepared
10) similarly
11) irrespective
12) incarnation
13) culturally
14) acknowledgement

Identifying Prefixes (p.142)

1) unrighteous
2) unbelievable
3) outrun
4) co-sponsor
5) multinational
6) unilateral
7) bicultural
8) unbelievable
9) undercurrent
10) unholy

Identifying Suffixes (p. 143)

1) multicultural (adjective)
2) holiness (noun)
3) spirituality (noun)
4) co-sponsorship (noun)
5) communicatively (adverb)
6) betrothal (noun)
7) Protestantism (noun)
8) orthodoxy (noun)
9) righteousness (noun)
10) justly (adverb)

➡ *Putting It All Together (p. 144)*

Word	Prefix	Root	Suffix	Part of Speech	Meaning
Example: unrighteous	un	right	eous	adjective	not doing right
undernourished	under	nourish	ed	adjective	lacking enough food
predestination	pre	destin	ation	noun	predetermined destiny
unpardonable	un	pardon	able	adjective	unforgivable
unfortunately	un	fortunate	ly	adverb	with negative consequences
regeneration	re	generat	ion	noun	new life

Appendix 1

Parables in the Gospels

The following is a list of the majority of Jesus' parables along with where they can be found in the gospels of Matthew, Mark, and Luke. The parables in bold are featured in this textbook. All of the parable titles listed are from the English Standard Version (ESV).

Nbr	Parable	Matthew	Mark	Luke
1	The Seed Growing		Mk 4:26-29	
2	**The Good Samaritan**			**Lk 10:25-37**
3	The Rich Fool			Lk 12:13-21
4	**The Sower**	**Mt 13:3-9**	**Mk 4:3-8**	**Lk 8:5-8**
5	The Weeds	Mt 13:24-30		
6	The Barren Fig Tree			Lk 13:6-9
7	The Mustard Seed	Mt 13:31-32	Mk 4:30-32	Lk 13:18-19
8	The Hidden Treasure	Mt 13:44		
9	The Pearl	Mt 13:45-46		
10	The Net	Mt 13:47-50		
11	The Lost Sheep	Mt 18:10-14		Lk 15:4-7
12	Unforgiving Servant	Mt 18:23-35		
13	The Lost Coin			Lk 15:8-10
14	**The Prodigal Son**			**Lk 15:11-32**
15	**The Dishonest Manager**			**Lk 16:1-13**
16	The Rich Man and Lazarus			Lk 16:19-31
17	**The Persistent Widow**			**Lk 18:1-8**
18	The Pharisee and the Tax Collector			Lk 18:9-14

19	Laborers in the Vineyard	Mt 20:1-16		
20	The Two Sons	Mt 21:28-32		
21	**The Wicked Tenants**	**Mt 21:33-44**	**Mk 12:1-11**	**Lk 20:9-18**
22	The Wedding Feast			Lk 14:7-11
23	**The Great Banquet**	**Mt 22:1-14**		**Lk 14:12-24**
24	The Lesson of the Fig Tree	Mt 24:32-35	Mk 13:28-31	Lk 21:29-33
25	The Ten Virgins	Mt 25:1-13		
26	**The Ten Minas**	**Mt 25:14-30**		**Lk 19:11-27**

Appendix 2

Abbreviations

Abbreviations for the books of the Bible as used in the English Standard Version (ESV).

The Old Testament

Genesis	Gn	Ecclesiastes	Eccl
Exodus	Ex	Song of Solomon	Sg
Leviticus	Lv	Isaiah	Is
Numbers	Nm	Jeremiah	Jer
Deuteronomy	Dt	Lamentations	Lam
Joshua	Jos	Ezekiel	Ez
Judges	Jgs	Daniel	Dn
Ruth	Ru	Hosea	Hos
1 Samuel	1 Sm	Joel	Jl
2 Samuel	2 Sm	Amos	Am
1 Kings	1 Kgs	Obadiah	Ob
2 Kings	2 Kgs	Jonah	Jon
1 Chronicles	1 Chr	Micah	Mi
2 Chronicles	2 Chr	Nahum	Na
Ezra	Ezr	Habakkuk	Hb
Nehemiah	Neh	Zephaniah	Zep
Esther	Est	Haggai	Hg
Job	Jb	Zechariah	Zec
Psalms	Ps	Malachi	Mal
Proverbs	Prv		

The New Testament

Matthew	Mt	1 Timothy	1 Tm
Mark	Mk	2 Timothy	2 Tm
Luke	Lk	Titus	Ti
John	Jn	Philemon	Phlm
Acts	Acts	Hebrews	Heb
Romans	Rom	James	Jas
1 Corinthians	1 Cor	1 Peter	1 Pt
2 Corinthians	2 Cor	2 Peter	2 Pt
Galatians	Gal	1 John	1 Jn
Ephesians	Eph	2 John	2 Jn
Philippians	Phil	3 John	3 Jn
Colossians	Col	Jude	Jude
1 Thessalonians	1 Thes	Revelation	Rv
2 Thessalonians	2 Thes		

Bibliography

Alter, Robert. *The Art of Biblical Narrative*, 2nd ed. New York: Basic Books, 2011.

Bahnsen, Greg. *Van Til's Apologetic: Readings and Analysis*. Philipsburg, NJ: P and R Publishing Company, 1998.

Berkhof, Louis. *Systematic Theology, Combined Edition*. Grand Rapids, MI: Eerdmans, 1996.

Billings, Todd J. *Union with Christ: Reframing Theology and Ministry for the Church*. Grand Rapids, MI: Baker Academic, 2011.

Blomberg, Craig L. *Interpreting the Parables*. Downers Grove, IL:InterVarsity, 1990.

Bock, Darrell L. *Luke: 9:51-24:53. Baker Exegetical Commentary on the New Testament*, Series, ed. Moises Silva. Grand Rapids, MI: Baker Books, 1994.

———. *Luke, The NIV Application Commentary*. Grand Rapids, MI: Zondervan, 1996.

Bowald, Mark A. "Grace" in Kevin J. Vanhoozer, ed., *Dictionary for Theological Interpretation of the Bible*. Grand Rapids, MI: Baker Academic, 2005.

Calvin, John. *Institutes of the Christian Religion*, ed. John T. McNeill, trans. Ford Lewis Battles. Louisville, KY: Westminster John Knox Press, 1960.

Carson, D.A. *The Difficult Doctrine of the Love of God*. Wheaton, IL: Crossway, 2000.

Fee, Gordon. *People of the Presence*. Podcast audio, Redeemer Sermon Store, MP3, October 15, 2010. http://sermons.redeemer.com/store/index.cfm?fuseaction=display&Product_ID=18591.

Frame, John M. *The Doctrine of the Knowledge of God*. Phillipsburg, NJ: Presbyterian and Reformed Publishing Company, 1987.

Green, Joel B. *The Gospel of Luke, New International Commentary on the New Testament* Series, ed. Gordon Fee. Grand Rapids, MI: Eerdmans, 1997.

Horton, Michael. *Introducing Covenant Theology*. Grand Rapids, MI: Baker Academic, 2006.

Keller, Timothy. *Center Church: Doing Balanced Gospel Ministry in Your City*. Grand Rapids, MI: Zondervan, 2012.

Keller, Timothy. *The Prodigal God*. New York, NY: Dutton, 2008.

———. *Writing from a Christian Worldview*, Podcast audio. Redeemer Sermon Store, MP3, March 31, 2013. http://sermons2.redeemer.com/sermons/writing-christian-worldviewhttp://sermons.redeemer.com/store/index.cfm?fuseaction=display&Product_ID=18591.

Kruse, Colin G. *Paul's Letter to the Romans. The Pillar New Testament Commentary* Series, ed. D.A. Carson. Grand Rapids, MI: Eerdmans, 2012.

Kuyper, Abraham. *Lectures on Calvinism*. Grand Rapids, MI: Eerdmans, 1931.

Lewis, C.S. *The Weight of Glory and Other Addresses*. New York, NY: Touchstone, 1996.

Lloyd-Jones, Sally. *The Jesus Storybook Bible: Every Story Whispers his Name*. Grand Rapids, MI: Zondervan, 2007.

Newbigen, Lesslie. *The Gospel in a Pluralistic Society*. Grand Rapids, MI: Eerdmans, 1989.

Oswalt, John N. *The Book of Isaiah. The New International Commentary on the Old Testament Series*. Grand Rapids, MI: Eerdmans, 1998.

Pao, David W. "Prophecy and Prophets in the NT" in Kevin J. Vanhoozer, ed., *Dictionary for Theological Interpretation of the Bible*. Grand Rapids, MI: Baker Academic, 2005.

Pao, David W. and Eckhard J. Schnabel, "Luke" in G.K. Beale and D.A. Carson, ed., *Commentary on the New Testament Use of the Old Testament*. Grand Rapids, MI: Baker Academic, 2007.

Patton, Michael Quinn. *Qualitative Evaluation and Research Methods 3rd Edition*. Newbury, CA: Sage Publications, 2002.

Philp, Jenefer, Rebecca Adams, and Noriko Iwashita. *Peer Interaction and Second Language Learning*. New York and London: Routledge, 2014.

Piper, John. *Desiring God: Meditations of a Christian Hedonist*. Portland, OR: Multnomah, 2003.

Poythress, Vern. *In the Beginning was the Word: Language – A God-Centered Approach*. Wheaton, IL: Crossway, 2009.

Reeves, Michael. *Delighting in the Trinity: An Introduction to the Christian Faith*. Downers Grove, IL: InterVarsity, 2012.

Snodgrass, Klyne. *Stories with Intent: A Comprehensive Guide to the Parables of Jesus*. Grand Rapids, MI: Eerdmans, 2008.

Vanhoozer, Kevin. *The Drama of Doctrine: A Canonical-Linguistic Approach to Christian Theology*. Louisville, KY: Westminster John Knox Press, 2005.

———. *Is There a Meaning in this Text?: The Bible, the Reader, and the Morality of Literary Knowledge*. Grand Rapids, MI: Zondervan, 1998.

Warfield, B.B. *The Plan of Salvation: Five Lectures delivered at Princeton School of Theology: June, 1914*. Philadelphia: Presbyterian Board of Publication, 1915.

Wilcock, Michael. *The Savior of the World: the Message of Luke's Gospel*. *The Bible Speaks Today* Series, ed. John Stott. Downers Grove, IL: InterVarsity Press, 1979.

Wolters, Albert. *Creation Regained: Biblical Basics for a Reformational Woldview, 2nd Edition*. Grand Rapids, MI: Eerdmans, 2005.

Wright, N.T. *The New Testament and the People of God*. Vol. 1 of *Christian Origins and the Question of God*. Minneapolis: Fortress Press, 1992.

Permissions

Permission was granted by the respective publishers for use of material from the following sources:

Alter, Robert. *The Art of Biblical Narrative*, 2nd ed. New York: ©copyright Basic Books, 2011.
Bock, Darrell L. *Luke, The NIV Application Commentary*. Grand Rapids, MI: ©copyright Zondervan, 1996.
Carson, D.A. *The Difficult Doctrine of the Love of God*. Wheaton, IL: ©copyright Crossway, 2000.
Keller, Timothy. *Center Church: Doing Balanced Gospel Ministry in Your City*. Grand Rapids, MI: ©copyright Zondervan, 2012.
Keller, Timothy. *The Prodigal God*. New York, NY: ©copyright Dutton, 2008.
Lewis, C.S. *The Weight of Glory*. ©copyright C.S. Lewis Pte Ltd, 1949.
Lloyd-Jones, Sally. *The Jesus Storybook Bible: Every Story Whispers his Name*. Grand Rapids, MI: ©copyright Zondervan, 2007.
Patton, Michael Quinn. *Qualitative Evaluation and Research Methods 3rd Edition*. Newbury, CA: ©copyright Sage Publications, 2002.
Poythress, Vern. *In the Beginning was the Word: Language – A God-Centered Approach*. Wheaton, IL: ©copyright Crossway, 2009.
Vanhoozer, Kevin. *Is There a Meaning in this Text?: The Bible, the Reader, and the Morality of Literary Knowledge*. Grand Rapids, MI: ©copyright Zondervan, 1998.
Wright, N.T. *The New Testament and the People of God*. Vol. 1 of *Christian Origins and the Question of God*. Minneapolis: ©copyright Fortress Press, 1992.

All other sources cited are considered fair use. No formal permission request was necessary.

Recommended Readings

References for English for Bible and Theology

Books

Dodd, Debbie. *Dictionary of Theological Terms in Simplified English.* Wheaton, IL: Evangelism and Mission Information Service (2003).

Pierson, Cheri. *Dictionary of Theological Terms in Simplified English Student Workbook.* Wheaton, IL: Evangelism and Mission Information Service (2003).

Pierson, Cheri, Dickerson, Lonna and Scott, Florence. *Exploring Theological English: Reading, Vocabulary and Grammar for ESL/EFL.*UK: Piquant Editions (2010).

Pierson, Cheri, Dickerson, Lonna and Scott, Florence. *Teacher's Guide: Exploring Theological English.* UK: Piquant Editions (2010).

Purgason, Kitty, ed. *English Teaching in Theological Contexts.* Pasadena, CA: William Carey Library (2010).

Sewell, Peter. *A Handbook of Theological English.* London: SPCK Publishing (1998).

Articles

Bankston, Will. "Global Theology in English: Promising or Problematic?" *The Gospel Coalition,* February 25, 2014, http://thegospelcoalition.org/blogs/tgc/2014/02/25/global-theology-in-english-promising-or-problematic/.

Pierson, Cheri and Bankston, Will. "English for Bible and Theology: Understanding and Communicating Theology Across Cultural and Linguistic Barriers." *Teaching Theology and Religion.*16:1 (January 2013). Blackwell Publishing, Ltd., 33-49.

Author Index

Langham Literature and its imprints are a ministry of Langham Partnership.

Langham Partnership is a global fellowship working in pursuit of the vision God entrusted to its founder John Stott –

to facilitate the growth of the church in maturity and Christ-likeness through raising the standards of biblical preaching and teaching.

Our vision is to see churches in the majority world equipped for mission and growing to maturity in Christ through the ministry of pastors and leaders who believe, teach and live by the Word of God.

Our mission is to strengthen the ministry of the Word of God through:

- nurturing national movements for biblical preaching
- fostering the creation and distribution of evangelical literature
- enhancing evangelical theological education

especially in countries where churches are under-resourced.

Our ministry

Langham Preaching partners with national leaders to nurture indigenous biblical preaching movements for pastors and lay preachers all around the world. With the support of a team of trainers from many countries, a multi-level programme of seminars provides practical training, and is followed by a programme for training local facilitators. Local preachers' groups and national and regional networks ensure continuity and ongoing development, seeking to build vigorous movements committed to Bible exposition.

Langham Literature provides majority world pastors, scholars and seminary libraries with evangelical books and electronic resources through grants, discounts and distribution. The programme also fosters the creation of indigenous evangelical books for pastors in many languages, through training workshops for writers and editors, sponsored writing, translation, strengthening local evangelical publishing houses, and investment in major regional literature projects, such as one volume Bible commentaries like *The Africa Bible Commentary*.

Langham Scholars provides financial support for evangelical doctoral students from the majority world so that, when they return home, they may train pastors and other Christian leaders with sound, biblical and theological teaching. This programme equips those who equip others. Langham Scholars also works in partnership with majority world seminaries in strengthening evangelical theological education. A growing number of Langham Scholars study in high quality doctoral programmes in the majority world itself. As well as teaching the next generation of pastors, graduated Langham Scholars exercise significant influence through their writing and leadership.

To learn more about Langham Partnership and the work we do visit **langham.org**

CPSIA information can be obtained
at www.ICGtesting.com
Printed in the USA
BVOW07s1845080517
483534BV00004B/162/P

9 781783 68940